JOHN L. SQUIRES

University of Utah

fun crafts for children

Prentice-Hall, Inc.   *Englewood Cliffs, N.J.*

PRENTICE-HALL INTERNATIONAL, INC., *London*
PRENTICE-HALL OF AUSTRALIA, PTY., LTD., *Sydney*
PRENTICE-HALL OF CANADA, LTD., *Toronto*
PRENTICE-HALL OF INDIA (PRIVATE) LIMITED, *New Delhi*
PRENTICE-HALL OF JAPAN, INC., *Tokyo*

Current printing (last digit):
13   12   11   10   9   8   7   6

© 1964 by PRENTICE-HALL, INC., Englewood Cliffs, N.J.

Library of Congress Catalog Card No.: 64-15596

PRINTED IN THE UNITED STATES OF AMERICA
34497-C

preface

This book was written with two important objectives in mind. The first purpose was to provide recreation leaders, teachers, and parents with a selected group of arts and crafts projects adapted to the recreational and educational needs of children of elementary school age. The second reason was to develop projects that are inexpensive, simple, and within the financial reach of participants and leaders.

For most children of elementary school age, participation in an arts and crafts program provided by a recreational institution is truly recreative. They voluntarily participate in the activity during their leisure for its own values. They not only enjoy making the project, but they wish to admire, appreciate, and use or play with the finished product. They especially enjoy projects which, when completed, have a practical use. Also, they are more easily interested in a program of arts and crafts which has this added attraction.

Only after careful consideration, and always keeping in mind the child's recreational objective, were the arts and crafts projects in this book selected. For the most part they were kept simple and useful while still presenting a manipulative challenge for the average child. They were selected because they had recreational, educational, useful and practical, as well as artistic values.

This book was prepared for the leader who needs a source of arts and crafts projects which are easy to understand and teach and which require very little financial outlay for materials and tools. Therefore, the more complicated and expensive arts and crafts projects, such as leather work, were not included in this book.

Most of the projects presented utilize materials and tools ordinarily found in the home, school, club, or playground. Many of them require scrap materials and, therefore, cost very little to make. Expensive materials and tools are factors which often deter leaders from presenting an arts and crafts program.

The author is indebted to the recreation leaders, elementary school teachers, parents, and other youth leaders who were students in his arts and crafts classes during the past fifteen years, and who, in their own arts and crafts classes experimented with these projects. Their valuable suggestions have greatly increased the usefulness of this book.

J.L.S.

contents

part one

**kindergarten and
first-grade ages   13**

Bookmarker   15
Butterfly   16
Christmas Decoration   17
Comic Picture
Transfers   18
Coolie Hat   19
Crayon-Ink Pictures   21
Crazy Animal Pic-
tures   22
Decoration Chain   23
Decorated Clothes
Sprinkler   24
Finger Painting   25
Flying Comet   27
Handy Sack Rack   28
Hummer-drummer   29
Milk-carton House
or Windmill   30

Paper-bag Hats   31
Paper-bag Halloween
Mask   32
Paper Candy Basket   33
Paper-plate Batik   34
Paper-plate Mask   35
Paper-plate Note or
Letter Holder   36
Peanut Finger Pup-
pets   37
Pincushion   38
Pinwheel   39
Plastic-spoon Dolls   40
Potato Stencil   41
Sachet Bag   42
Sailboat   43
Sewing or Scrap
Basket   44
Silhouette or Profile
Picture   45
Single-line Checker-
board   46
Sound Magnifier   47

Sponge Stenciling   48
Stand-up Double
Animals   49
String Painting   51
Tell Me About It   52
Twine Holder   53
Twirling Colored Disk   54
The Whirligig   55
Wooden-spoon Book
Marker   56
Woolly Lamb   57

part two

second-grade ages   59

Artwork envelope   61
Balloon Figures   62
Christmas Chain   63
Color Twirler   64
Cork Sailboat   65
Cork Toys, Animals,
or Figures   66
Crazy Racing Roller   67

Cutout Name Design   68
Cutout Pictures—
Cloth   69
Decorated Paper Clip   70
Fish Aquarium   71
Flower Vase (Yarn)   72
Indian Headdress   73
Indian Tepee   74
Jet Plane   75
Paper-bag Bird   76
Paper-bag Snowman   77
Plastic-foam Man   78
Record Flower Pot   79
Rock Paperweights   80
Sack Puppet   81
Salt Beads   82
Snip and Art   83
Spool Rack   84
Spool Top   85
Star Snowflake   86
Stick Horse   87
Stocking Puppets   88
String Key Chain   89

Tin-can Stilts	90	Glitter Vase	113
Tin-can Telephone		Hobbyhorse	114
System	91	Indian Rattle	115
Torn-paper Pictures	92	Kite	116
Tube Puppet	93	Moving-shadow	
Yarn Basket	94	Figures	118

part three

third-grade ages 97

Aluminum-foil		Paper Beads	119
Picture	99	Parachute	120
Belt Weaving	101	Peanut Man	121
Bright-button		Plaster Picture	
Picture	102	Frame	122
Buttonhole Puzzle	103	Powered Houseboat	123
Buzzy Bee	104	Propelled Boat	124
Colored-salt Picture	105	Ring Toss	125
Cord Holder	106	Spatter Painting	126
Crayon-Eraser		Spool Knitting	127
Picture	107	Stocking Hand	
Crepe-paper Basket	108	Puppets	129
Doll or Puppet Hat	110	Stuffed Rubber Doll	130
Egg-carton Cater-		Tambourine	131
pillar	111	Willow Whistle	132
Egg-cup Tulips	112		

part four

fourth-grade ages 135

Acrobat	137

Beanie Cap	139	Frame	167
Bug Cage	140	Snapshot Holder	168
Case for Glasses,		Spool Animals	170
Pens, or Pencils	141	Spool Penholder	171
Confetti or Torn-		Sword Pins	172
paper Pictures	142	Table Croquet	174
Decorated Puzzle		Wheel Runner	175
Sticks	143	Wrapped Wire or	
Dyed-rice Mosaic	146	Rod Figures	176
Earth Weather			
Satellite	148		
Fish Kite	150		

part five

fifth-grade ages 177

Handy Miniature		Black Walnut Belt	
Scorekeeper	152	or Hatband	179
Hot Pad	153	Carton Hats	181
Jitterbugs	155	Christmas Wreath	182
Lighthouse	156	Clothes-hanger	
Log Cabin	157	Bookend	184
Paper-napkin Holder	159	Crayon Stenciling	185
Papier-mâché Pup-		Crazy-quilt Vase	186
pets or Dolls	160	Fluffy-paper Vase	187
Pencil Holder	162	Flying Propeller	188
Rope Belt	163	Girl's Wrist Purse	189
Rubber-headed		Glass Inking	190
Drum	165	Handy Pants Hanger	191
Rustic Picture			

Inlaid Checkerboard 192
Inlaid Serving Tray 193
Jack-in-the-box 194
Matching Dolls 196
Moving Flip-top
Faces 198
Painted Drinking
Glass 199
Papier-mâché Piggy
Bank 200
Peek-a-vue 202
See Seeds Grow 203
Simple String Chain 204
Soap Carving 205
Spool Dolls 206

Tie Rack 207
Twisted-crepe-paper
Vase 208
Wriggly Dragon 209

part six
sixth-grade ages 211

Box-of-many-faces 213
Christmas Candles 215
Crepe-paper Lei 216
Elusive Elastic Trick 217
Foam Pins and
Ornaments 219
Folded Newspaper

Hat 220
Folded Tissue Car-
nation 222
Identification Tag 223
Lively Mouse 224
Marble Bag or Girl's
Purse 226
Marble Game 229
Miniature Bowling
Blocks 231
Miniature Shuffle-
board 232
Mystery Wheel 234
Paper Tree 236
Perpetual Motion

Sunray Motor 237
Plaster of Paris
Splash 239
Reading Stand 241
Rickrack earrings 242
Schoolbook Strap 243
Spool Tractor 244
Tippy 245
Walnut-shell Picture 246
Wire Necklace or
Belt 247
Yarn Ball, Method
One 249
Yarn Ball, Method
Two 250

introduction

Since his advent on earth, man has expressed an urge to use his hands to create many things. However, past records prove that he was never satisfied just to make an article, but he desired to express his aesthetic nature in the finished product. He constructed a practical clay vessel but did not seem completely satisfied in the pleasure he received in making it just for its usefulness. He usually attempted to express an aesthetic urge by making the vessel smooth, even of line, pleasing to the eye, and then by coloring and decorating it with artistic imagination and ability.

Man, the intellectual being that he is, also has the anatomical ability to manipulate his fingers and thumbs to his advantage. He is able to touch his thumb to his fingers as no other animal can. They work together as a manipulative tool, which makes it possible for him to fashion and to create in detail an intricate object that reflects his craftsmanship and aesthetic nature. Man not only has the anatomical and mental ability to do and make, but he possesses, along with this gift, a manipulative urge that he constantly seeks to satisfy.

In the past much of man's work and play required that he use his manipulative ability to hand-fashion much of what he needed. Today, very few men work with their hands, but they still possess the ability and the urge to create. Some of them satisfy this desire by developing hobbies and by working around the yard and in the home. Their sons and daughters are being denied the satisfaction of creating by hand. Almost everything they want is handed to them as a finished product. Little opportunity exists for most of our youth to paint, decorate, or create with their hands.

There is a great need to help youth participate in a rich program of arts and crafts. The challenge is to develop their skills and interests so that they can continue throughout their lives to participate in worthwhile and satisfying arts and crafts activities that will enrich their lives and help satisfy their aesthetic and manipulative inclinations.

youth in the program

Most children desire to participate in an arts and crafts program because they enjoy the actual making of the project. They also seek other objectives:

1. To be with others in a social situation and be accepted by them and by the leader
2. To have leadership in an activity that is socially approved and a profitable use of their time
3. To receive recognition for a project well done
4. To improve skills, coordination, and understanding

1

5. To have an opportunity for self-expression
6. To enjoy the feeling of satisfaction upon completion of a project
7. To be able to admire, use, or play with the finished product

the leader in the program

Leadership is the ability to get others to participate dynamically in an activity, to reach an objective. It involves using methods for the introduction, motivation, initiation, evaluation, and maintenance of an activity. The more effective the action is toward the objective, the better the leadership. Activity always has an objective, and it must have leadership. Therefore, activity, leadership, and objectives are related, intrinsic, and interactive one with the other. As quickly as one situation changes, so the other elements change. A teacher or a recreation leader, in keeping with this concept, must understand objectives, methods, people, activities, and situations.

leadership objectives

The leader in the arts and crafts program has recreative and educative objectives. His generalized objective can be stated as: The leadership of people in arts and crafts activities for enjoyment, development, and adjustment according to standards.

1. *Leadership* is an objective because it motivates, guides, and gives purpose to the activity. It can determine the quality of the participation.
2. *Enjoyment* of the participants is an objective of the leader because it is one of the primary objectives of his followers and therefore one of the important reasons for presenting the activity. It also determines whether the activity will be continued with enthusiasm and whether it will be recreative for the participant.
3. *Development* is an educational objective of the arts and crafts leader. The good leader looks beyond the enjoyment-recreative objective and purposely strives to develop within his followers proper interests, favorable attitudes, worthy ideals, and healthy emotions. He works to develop the minds of his participants, to increase their knowledge, understanding, and interpretation concerning the activity. He teaches skills and helps to develop the proper and required coordination needed to complete the project.
4. *Adjustment* is an educational objective of the leader. He leads the participants in solving the problems of their environment. He recognizes the need for youth to adjust and to solve the problems of their environment, and he knows that those who fail to make the proper adjustments are frustrated and unhappy at their failure to adjust. In order to obtain the proper atmosphere for good participation, he guides and

assists his followers in making proper adjustments with themselves and others, the surrounding conditions, and the activity itself. The making of proper adjustments by youth in the arts and crafts program not only increases their enjoyment of the activity, but also can carry over into their lives and help them to live and enjoy a more adequate and effective existence.

The arts and crafts environment involves making adjustments to the following:

(a) *Laws*—obeying and following rules and regulations.
(b) *Concepts*—making correct interpretations and understandings concerning the activity.
(c) *Protection*—learning how to protect oneself and others in the activity so as to enjoy it without accidents or injury to health or morals.
(d) *Movement*—moving about in a way that will not interfere with other participants, and using tools correctly and efficiently, such as properly manipulating or moving a wood plane or sanding in the correct direction, and so forth.
(e) *Communication*—learning how to express oneself properly so as to be understood and to be able to understand others. The specific vocabulary of the arts and crafts field must be understood to make the proper communicative adjustment.
(f) *Sociability*—helping each participant feel wanted so that he will enjoy and participate in the sociable atmosphere that should be present under good leadership.
(g) *Finances*—asking each participant to stay within his financial means when purchasing tools and materials.
(h) *Recreation*—learning to make and enjoy an arts and crafts project for the sake of the activity itself and to avoid making the activity a "wreck-reation." This is a hard adjustment for some people to make.
(i) *Sex Relationships*—reacting properly to those of the opposite and of the same sex.
(j) *Surroundings*—selecting and making suitable projects from available resources, varied according to the area in which the participants live. At camp, the projects could be made from the natural materials found in the area, and at school or recreation centers the projects could be related to and supplement the educational or recreational program.

5. *Standards* are educative and recreative objectives of the leaders and participants. Since standards are measurements of quality, the leader should use them to help improve the quality of the projects completed by the participants in the arts and crafts program. The supreme function of a leader is to set the standards in the activity and to develop within his follow-

3

ers the desire to reach these standards. A good leader uses standards as a guide to measure and evaluate the quality of his leadership methods and the quality of the educative and recreative objectives of the program.

standards in leadership

Leadership involves the development and organization of methods to motivate, introduce, and maintain the program. The leader motivates prospective followers to enter the activity, and once they are initiated into the activity, he seeks to motivate their remaining until its completion. The leader appeals to the participants through methods that attract their attention, arouse their interest or curiosity, and challenge their ability and lift them to high achievement in the activity. The recreative enjoyment objective of the participant is important and should be stimulated with enthusiasm before, during, and after the activity. To help reach this objective the activities selected should be adapted to the needs and abilities of the participants. Methods of presentation are used that assist the followers in understanding their task and in completing it successfully according to high standards. The participants are made to feel wanted in the activity by the leader and other participants. The leader, through personal leadership qualities and organizational methods and techniques, be-

comes the guiding force around which the activity continues.

Personal leadership qualities and organizational methods needed for motivating, introducing, and maintaining an arts and crafts program are:

1. Personal leadership qualities
   (a) A happy and pleasing disposition
   (b) A deep interest in people and activity
   (c) Confidence in one's own ability
   (d) Fairness, honesty, and consideration of others
   (e) Emotional control
   (f) Respect for others and an impersonal approach
   (g) Energy, enthusiasm, and an understanding of the activity
   (h) A pleasing voice and no disturbing mannerisms
   (i) An informal attitude without sarcasm or dogmatic action
   (j) A sense of humor
   (k) Skill, strength, and endurance
2. Organizational methods involving participants
   (a) The leader allows group freedom in an informal atmosphere. He allows participants to select the group with which they would like to sit and work. The informal groups are allowed to visit, talk, and converse freely with one another. Enjoyable merriment and noise is allowed if it grows from the activity itself and does not inter-

fere with the quality and progress of the project.

(b) He avoids such formal procedures as blowing a shrill whistle for attention, calling role, and other disturbing and noisy methods.

(c) As much as possible he eliminates formal lining up and marching to obtain materials or tools and avoids strict rules and regulations of conduct that stifle the atmosphere of fun and enjoyment.

(d) The seats and tables are arranged to prevent confusion and to give each participant elbow room and clear vision of the leader and the demonstrations. Seating arrangements should facilitate the work of the participants and increase the efficiency of the leader.

(e) All arts and crafts groups should be kept small because most participants need careful individual guidance.

3. Organizational methods involving the activity

(a) The introduction is made short and simple. Several finished samples of the project are shown. They are demonstrated as to usefulness, the fun to be had in making them, and an idea of what the finished project can be like. These samples should be used only as guides and should not interfere with the child's originality and personality.

(b) The group is initiated into the activity quickly. Very little time should be wasted in talking. The leader must keep in mind that the participants are eager to start the activity. After the brief talk, the first step is explained and the participants start work immediately.

(c) After each step is explained, the leader should give special attention to the progress of each individual and help those having difficulty. If he finds that most of them are confused or confronted with the same difficulties, it is usually best to stop the group and reteach the technique on a group level. However, if the technique is really difficult, individual guidance methods are necessary. This is one of the reasons for keeping arts and crafts groups small.

(d) The leader should practice using the tools and making the project until he can skillfully demonstrate the techniques and show the participants how to proceed successfully. The practice involved in making the display develops the needed skill and gives insight as to what problems the participants will face.

(e) A step-by-step method of presentation is required for most arts and crafts projects, proceeding only as the group can complete each step successfully. Do not move so fast that the slower participants become lost, nor so slowly that boredom develops among the more efficient workers. Sometimes it is good practice to use the better workers to help others in the group. This keeps the group together and helps the development of leadership and friendship among the participants.

(f) Methods for improving the interests, attitudes, ideals, and emotions of the participants toward the activity should be developed.

4. Organizational methods involving facilities

(a) All tools needed for the activity should be ready for use. They should be in first-rate condition, conveniently placed, and of sufficient number for the group.

(b) All tools should be placed in a central location and should be clearly marked with the owner's or organization's name.

(c) When not in use, scarce tools should be returned to their proper place.

(d) At the end of the class, all tools should be cleaned by the participants and put away.

(e) Each participant should be taught how to use each tool properly.

(f) Work tables should be covered with newspaper to protect their surfaces from damage.

(g) Each participant should be responsible for keeping his working area clean. At the close of the activity, he should clean his area, put away his project, tools, and materials. Neatness of work and area should be emphasized by the leader.

(h) Participants and leaders should wear clothing that allows them to work freely with tools and materials. They should protect their clothing from becoming soiled or damaged.

(i) Waste baskets and trash cans should be conveniently located.

(j) Materials and supplies needed in making a project should be conveniently placed or delivered to the participants to prevent confusion and to guarantee that each one receives his share.

(k) All dangerous tools should be used only by the leader or under his strict supervision.

5. Organization of the time schedule

(a) Because of the nature of children it is usually best to establish a time schedule so that most of the projects can be completed in one class period. This is especially true when working with groups in which attendance is not stable. However, with more stable groups the leader can purposely start with projects that can be completed in one sitting and, as the attention span lengthens, lengthen the projects.

(b) Classes should be conveniently time-scheduled and arranged so that the participants are able to attend at least two classes per week.

(c) Class periods should not be too long. If a project requires more than 90 minutes, it is usually best to postpone its completion until the next class.

Leaders who use simple projects that require no more than one hour for completion usually are more successful.

(d) To attain the participant's recreative objectives, the time schedule should allow for rest periods and time for playing with the finished project.

6. Organization of the protective program

(a) The leader has the responsibility of averting all forces that might be detrimental or injurious to the health, morals, aesthetic nature, and thinking of the participants. Especially in the recreational setting, the success of the protective program many times determines whether or not the activity will commence or be continued. The parents of the children help to make these decisions. Few parents will knowingly allow their children to attend recreational programs if they feel the leader will not establish standards that will at all times protect their children. Many recreational programs have been discontinued because parents became alarmed at the things their children were learning and saying about the program, or that they were using profanity, drawing "dirty" pictures, running around with bad company, learning misconceptions, or had contacted a communicable disease. Many times an outbreak of a communicable disease, such as ringworm or mumps, will cause parents to withdraw their children from a recreational program. Parents always think about protection before allowing their children to attend any program. In fact, as the first requirement of satisfying their peace of mind, parents always want to know if a leader will be present to protect their children. Parents must have confidence in the leader and his standards of protection.

(b) Methods should be developed to protect the participants from accidents and injuries. Dangerous tools should be used carefully and only under proper leadership. Machines should have safety guards. Wiring should be inspected and kept in good repair. Tools that are broken and dangerous should be discarded. Trash should not be allowed to pile up on floors. Inflammable materials should be stored away from heat and in proper containers. Chairs and work tables should be safe and strong.

(c) Dangerous projects such as rock-propelling or arrow-shooting instruments should be avoided in the program.

(d) Participants should be taught proper protective attitudes and interests, group consciousness, and methods to protect themselves and others from injury.

(e) In case of an accident, previously arranged methods for caring for the injured should be available and used.

(f) Ventilation, light, and heat should be adjustable to protect the health of the participants.

(g) Pure drinking water and clean, efficient toilet facilities are needed, and rest periods should be provided.

(h) Work tables and chairs should be at proper heights and comfortable for participants.

(i) The leader should eliminate participants from the program who show signs of illness or of having a communicable disease.

(j) The work area and the building should be in good repair and neatly kept so as to appear attractive to participants and not degrading to their aesthetic nature.

(k) The leader of the arts and crafts projects should emphasize neatness and originality of line and color to increase and develop the aesthetic and artistic nature of the participants.

(l) The leader should base all statements upon facts and should correct misconceptions and misunderstandings of the participants. He should discourage the use of amulets, signs, statements, or ideas based upon superstitions or false information.

(m) The leader should develop methods to protect morals of the participants. He should set an example through clean living and proper moral conduct. He should correct improper relationships, curb profanity, cheating, stealing, dishonesty, and other undesirable personal actions of participants.

supplementary and useful information for the leader

flexibility of projects

After considerable classroom experimentation and testing, the arts and crafts projects were classified and arranged and presented in this book according to elementary school grade levels. However, this does not mean that they are only suitable for the specific grade level for which they are presented. Most of the projects throughout the book can be simplified or made more complex to meet the educational and recreational needs of children at any age or grade level. The arrangement of the projects according to school grades is for convenience only and does not mean to indicate that the projects are only for school teachers. They are equally valuable for parents and for all types of recreation leaders.

organization of projects

Each project in the book follows the same format. The special materials and tools required are listed first, but general or common things, such as pencils, rulers, scissors, pins, and needles, are sometimes not listed, because so many projects require their use that space is saved by not repeating them throughout the book. However, a list is provided in this chapter naming all the common tools that are not generally listed for each project but understood as needed and ordinarily available. They are the minimum tools required to do simple arts and crafts.

How to make all projects is explained briefly but fully under "Procedure." The directions are concise and simply worded.

The illustrations and diagrams coincide with the statements under "Procedure." The wording accompanying the figures is simple and concise. For example, instead of saying "Fold down the flap," it will state briefly "fold down"—with or without an arrow showing direction. However, the procedures are usually more specific because they supplement the drawings.

For most projects, no statement concerning their use is given. This information is not needed because leaders can elaborate and explain to their groups how to use the projects. *How the participants use the finished project will depend upon the motivation of the leader.* Whenever a project requires an idea or skill previously described and illustrated, a reference to the necessary information is given. For example, "Make a star and decorate it with glitter." The star is a separate project in the book; therefore it will be referred to only for your information. If one does not know how to make a star, he need only turn to the reference and follow the directions. Referral and other space-saving methods are used to permit the inclusion of a greater number of illustrations and projects.

Procedures do not include teaching suggestions; each leader will develop his own teaching methods through making and completing his own samples of the project. A leader, while making his teaching samples, will have little need for a discussion of teaching techniques to help him guide the participants. Of course, the procedures are, in themselves, teaching suggestions because they follow step by step the development of each project.

The following tools are needed in making many of the projects and are listed here for reference, and usually are not listed again under "tools" for each project.

1. Pencil
2. Ruler
3. Eraser
4. Scissors
5. Knife or razor blade
6. Sewing needles and threads
7. Colors—crayons, water colors, poster paints
8. Paste
9. Glue—plastic cement and regular
10. Water color brushes
11. Small paint brush, ½ in. wide
12. Ink and felt stick dry ink markers

The following is a list of usable scraps and other materials.

Beads
Beans
Belt buckles
Belts—leather, cloth, plastic
Boxes—cardboard, candy, medicine, cigar, packing, etc.
Broom handles
Buttons—all sizes and colors
Cardboard—discarded posters
Cartons—cottage cheese, ice cream, milk, cereal
Cord
Corks
Cotton
Cloth materials—felt, silk, rayon, wool, cotton, oil, plastic, etc.
Clothes pins
Elastic bands
Envelopes
Feathers—all types
Foam—insulation, plastic, styrafoam

Furs—all types
Hats
Hose—ladies' nylons
Jar rings and lids
Jewelry—costume
Magazines
Marbles
Matches—wooden, used
Metal washers or bolt nuts
Nails—all kinds and sizes
Newspapers
Paints and varnishes
Paper—butcher, wrapping, art, construction, plastic, tissue, wall, Christmas wrapping, carbon, colored, metallic, etc.
Paper clips
Paraffin
Phonograph records
Pins—straight, hair, bobby, hat, safety, etc.
Pipe cleaners
Plates—paper, aluminum foil
Pop bottle caps

Popsickle sticks
Razor blades
Ribbons
Rice
Rickrack
Rope
Rubber inner tubes
Sacks—paper, wax paper, plastic, cloth
Sandpaper
Screen
Sequins and glitter
Shells—egg, peanut, walnut, sea

Sox—men's, bobby
Spools—all sizes
Spoons—wooden, plastic
Sponges—animal, plastic
Steel wool
String
Tacks
Tin cans
Toothpicks
Wire
Wire clothes hangers
Wood scraps—all kinds and sizes
Yarns

Most scrap materials used in the projects can be found in or around the home. Scrap wood usually can be obtained without cost from a lumber yard and plywood from a cabinet shop. Many upholstery shops are willing to give away scrap materials. This is also true of plastic materials and leatherette, valuable substitutes for leather. Cigar boxes can be obtained from drugstores. Gasoline stations and garages will usually supply old distributor heads or damaged inner tubes for elastics, drum tops, and stuffed dolls. Sample books full of beautifully colored paper sheets can be obtained from wallpaper stores. Tailor shops and stores selling fabrics are valuable sources for scrap materials.

terms and meanings

1. *Cut* means to use a knife or razor blade.
2. *Clip* means to use scissors.
3. A *dotted line* usually means fold.
4. Cut or clip lines are solid and marked "cut" or "clip."
5. *Paste* means to use some type of wheat paste. This paste is usually white and is suitable only for jobs requiring little adhesiveness.
6. *Glue* means to use a strong adhesive such as LePage's Glue, Elmer's Glue-All, or a similar product.
7. *Fast-drying glue* is a plastic glue that dries in a few seconds.
8. *Sand* means to rub with sandpaper and to go with the grain when working on wood.

11

part one   kindergarten and first-grade ages

kindergarten and first-grade ages

Bookmarker 15	Flying Comet 27	Peanut Finger Puppets 37	Sound Magnifier 47
Butterfly 16	Handy Sack Rack 28	Pincushion 38	Sponge Stenciling 48
Christmas Decoration 17	Hummer-drummer 29	Pinwheel 39	Stand-up Double Animals 49
Comic Picture Transfers 18	Milk-carton House or Windmill 30	Plastic-spoon Dolls 40	String Painting 51
Coolie Hat 19	Paper-bag Hats 31	Potato Stencil 41	Tell Me About It 52
Crayon-Ink Pictures 21	Paper-bag Halloween Mask 32	Sachet Bag 42	Twine Holder 53
Crazy Animal Pictures 22	Paper Candy Basket 33	Sailboat 43	Twirling Colored Disk 54
Decoration Chain 23	Paper-plate Batik 34	Sewing or Scrap Basket 44	The Whirligig 55
Decorated Clothes Sprinkler 24	Paper-plate Mask 35	Silhouette or Profile Picture 45	Wooden-spoon Bookmarker 56
Finger Painting 25	Paper-plate Note or Letter Holder 36	Single-line Checkerboard 46	Woolly Lamb 57

bookmarker

materials and tools

Plain envelope, piece of string or ribbon, magazine with colored pictures, glue.

procedure

1. Cut lower corner from envelope about 2½ in. on each side. You may wish to scallop it (Figs. 1 and 2).
2. Decorate or glue a small picture to the triangle (Fig. 2).
3. Glue string or ribbon on inside of triangle so it comes out at the corner (Fig. 3).
4. Place triangle over upper corner of book and place ribbon in between pages to hold your place (Fig. 4).

average time required

10 minutes

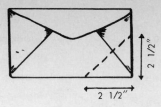

Fig. 1

Fig. 2

Glue

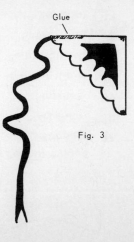

Fig. 3

ARTS AND Crafts

Fig. 4

butterfly

materials and tools

Brightly colored crepe paper, needle and thread, scissors, strip of paper, fine wire, crayons.

procedure

1. Cut a butterfly shape from the crepe paper (Fig. 1).
2. Pinch out the side edges into tiny ruffles. Bend the wire into a hairpin shape and then thread the wire up through the body of the butterfly. Gather up the crepe paper as shown in Fig. 2. At the top of the butterfly's body, twist the two ends of the wire together to form the antennae.
3. Cover the gathers with a strip of paper cut into the shape of a butterfly's body. Decorate center paper with crayons to resemble the body of a butterfly (Fig. 3).

average time required

30 minutes. Butterflies are easy to make and appropriate for children. They are too difficult, however, for the average preschool child to make, but he would enjoy playing with them. They make very colorful and attractive decorations.

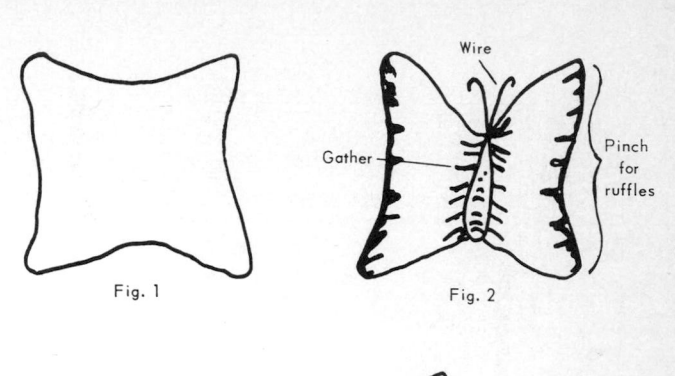

Fig. 1

Fig. 2

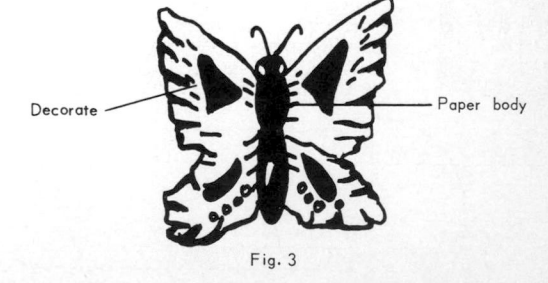

Fig. 3

christmas decoration

materials and tools

Colored or metallic paper, scissors, ruler, needle, thread, pencil, string.

procedure

1. Cut out six circles from colored paper all about 8 in. in diameter. Use more circles if a fluffier decoration is desired.
2. Fold each circle three times. The folded circle now resembles a cone (Fig. 1). One side of the cone has three folded edges showing. Clip these edges irregularly to give a lacy appearance when opened (Fig. 1).
3. Open the circle and cut the other four fold lines to within ½ in. of the center of the circle as shown in Fig. 2.
4. Fold on the lacy edges. Fold sections opposite to one another. Fold the sides of the first section down and the side of the next section up, etc. (Fig. 3).
5. String the circles one after another on a string. The string is threaded through the center of each circle. Push the circles tightly to the end of the string and tie in place. Spread and fluff them out and you have Christmas balls (Fig. 4).

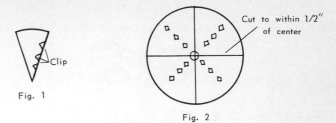

average time required

45 minutes

Clip

Fig. 1

Cut to within 1/2″
of center

Fig. 2

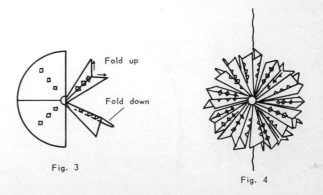

Fold up
Fold down

Fig. 3

Fig. 4

comic picture transfers

materials and tools

Comic strips, paraffin, white paper, spoon.

procedure

1. Rub a film of paraffin wax on a piece of white paper.
2. Place the waxed surface against the comic strip picture you wish to transfer.
3. Rub firmly on the back of the white paper with the flat part of a spoon until the picture that is against the waxed side has transferred (Figs. 1 and 2).
4. Frame the transferred picture with colored paper.

average time required

10 minutes

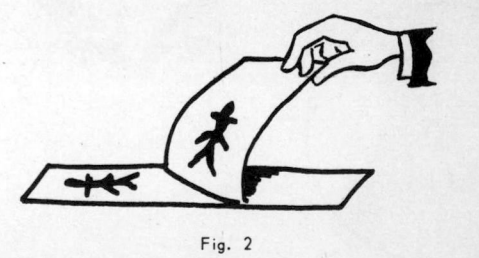

Fig. 1

Fig. 2

coolie hat

materials and tools

Wallpaper or heavy wrapping paper, water colors or crayons or colored paper, cord or yarn, ribbon or raffia, four gummed stickers or glue, light cardboard for reinforcements, shellac, paste, small paint brush for applying shellac.

procedure

1. On the wallpaper or wrapping paper draw a circle with a 10-in. radius.
2. Cut out the circle.
3. Make a slit from the outside edge of the circle to its center (Fig. 1).
4. On the outside of the hat draw, paint, or paste a design. If wallpaper is used, its own design is sufficient.
5. Overlap the slit edges a few inches and paste in place. (If very heavy material is used, staple in place.) (Fig. 2).
6. Six inches from the edge of the hat on both sides cut or punch a hole (Fig. 1).
7. On the inside of the hat reinforce the holes with cardboard squares or gummed stickers.
8. Braid cord or yarn into desired lengths and insert ends into the holes. Tie knots in the ends of the straps. Leave the loose ends as tassels (Fig. 3).

19

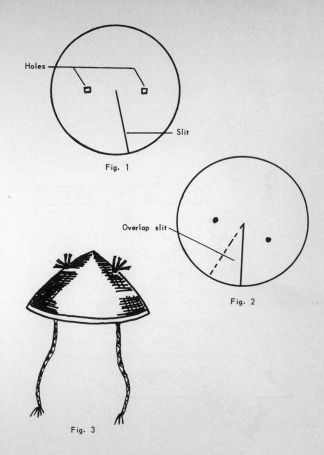

Fig. 1

Holes

Slit

Overlap slit

Fig. 2

Fig. 3

9. If shellac is applied to the hat, it will be much more durable.

average time required

40 minutes, depending upon how elaborately decorated. All age groups can make this project with varying degrees of help from the teacher. Basically, this is a very easy project, but young children will need a pattern; older children can make their own.

crayon-ink pictures

Fig. 1

materials and tools

Heavy paper or poster cardboard, crayons, black india ink, water color brush, bobby pin or any pointed instrument.

procedure

1. Place the piece of paper on the table and color with crayons. Use any colors desired and completely cover the paper with several colors (Fig. 1).
2. Completely cover the crayon scribbling with ink and let it dry thoroughly.
3. To make a picture or design scratch the black ink off with a bobby pin. As the ink comes off, the brilliant colors will appear. The result is surprising and fascinating (Fig. 2).

average time required

40 minutes. Instead of using india ink, you may apply a heavy coat of black or purple crayon or poster paint.

Fig. 2

21

crazy animal pictures

materials and tools

One sheet of manila paper, 12 by 18 in., assorted cloth (printed or plain), paper scraps, buttons, pipe cleaners, old jewelry, and so forth.

procedure

1. Cut out from cloth and paper scraps the background for the picture and arrange upon the foundation paper (clouds, trees, etc.) (Fig. 1).
2. Cut out from cloth or paper scraps an imaginary animal and arrange on foundation paper (Fig. 2).
3. When materials have been arranged as desired, glue them one at a time to the foundation paper (Fig. 3).
4. The object of this project is to create an imaginary animal from the scraps and to make up a story to fit the animal picture.

average time required

30 minutes

Fig. 1

Fig. 2

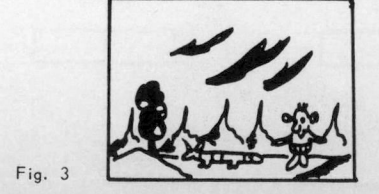

Fig. 3

decoration chain

materials and tools

Colored paper, paste or glue.

procedure

1. Cut out several narrow strips of paper about 8 in. long by ½ in. wide (Fig. 1).
2. Put a small amount of paste on one of the paper ends (Fig. 2).
3. Fold the other end around to make a circle or hoop (Fig. 3).
4. To make the chain, place one end of a strip of paper through the previous link before gluing it together (Fig. 4).

average time required

40 minutes. The length of the strip of paper determines the size of the links. Increase or decrease the width or length as desired.

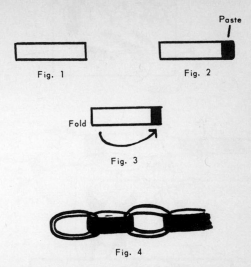

Paste

Fig. 1   Fig. 2

Fold

Fig. 3

Fig. 4

decorated clothes sprinkler

materials and tools

A medium-sized pop bottle, clothes sprinkler nozzle, desired decorations.

procedure

1. Put nozzle in top of bottle.
2. Paint the bottle with enamel and be sure to let the paint dry before using. Paste pictures from a magazine on the bottle, or paint your own design.
3. If you use picture decorations, you should shellac or varnish the finished product.

average time required

30 minutes

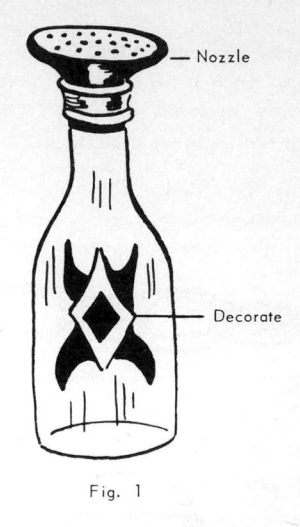

Fig. 1

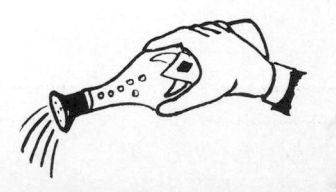

24

finger painting

materials and tools

Finger paint, paper, water.

recipe

1 cup glossy starch
¼ cup soap flakes, if desired

Add cold water (enough to dissolve the starch) to the starch and mix. Then add two cups of hot water and, stirring constantly, boil until the mixture becomes clear. A little water may be added if the mixture becomes too thick. Powder paint may be added to the mixture, or a small amount of powder paint may be sprinkled on the starch after some has been put on the paper.

procedure

1. Wet the paper, either by dipping it in cold water or by sprinkling a small amount of water on it (Fig. 1). Use paper that will not get soggy. A good paper to use is butcher paper or shelf-lining paper.
2. Apply the finger paint to the paper and spread it around. Now go to work. The hands, fingers, arms, and elbows all are usable in finger painting (Fig. 2).

3. Place the picture flat to dry. A warm iron may be used on the back side of the paper to smooth it out. Hang the painting on the wall.

variations

Use a cardboard comb with notches of various sizes to make designs. Put three or four colors (light to dark) in horizontal bands or blotches across the paper and swirl the comb or fingers through them. Bold plaids can be made by drawing the comb across the paper horizontally and then vertically. Finger paintings may also be used as book covers, Christmas wrapping paper, flower-pot covering, etc.

alternate recipes

Deluxe Finger Paint

⅓ cup glossy starch   ½ cup soap flakes
2 cups boiling water   2 teaspoons glycerine
                            Vegetable dye

Dissolve the starch in a little cold water; then add boiling water and stir well until it is clear and smooth. Add soap flakes and stir well until dissolved. Remove from heat, add glycerine, and stir. Add dye and stir. This paint will keep indefinitely if stored in a covered jar.

White Flour Finger Paint

1 cup flour	3 cups water
½ cup sugar	1 tablespoon boric acid
	1 teaspoon cinnamon oil

Mix the flour, sugar, and 1 cup of water together and place in a double boiler. Cook until thick and then add the remaining 2 cups of water and continue cooking. Stir slowly and add 1 tablespoon boric acid when cooked. To make especially pleasing, add 1 teaspoon of cinnamon oil.

Wheat Paste Finger Paint

Wheat paste	Water
	Paint (cold water variety)

Fill your container with desired amount of hot water and gradually pour in wheat paste until you reach the proper thickness. Stir well to work out all the lumps. Add colored cold water paint to the paste.

Finger Paint with Talcum Powder

¾ cup laundry starch	¼ cup talcum powder
3½ cups boiling water	Dry paint or food coloring
¾ cup soap flakes	

Mix the starch with a little cold water until it becomes creamy. Add the boiling water and cook until the mixture becomes clear.

Stir constantly. Add talcum powder. Allow the mixture to cool a bit; then add the soap flakes and stir. Divide into jars and stir in the colors. Keep covered.

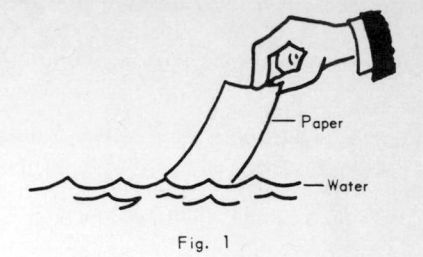

Fig. 1

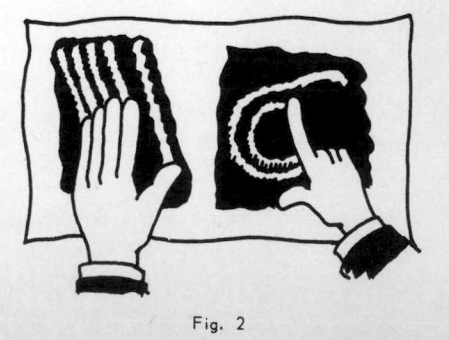

Fig. 2

flying comet

materials and tools

Long-shaped rubber balloon, string, small piece of cork 1 in. long and with a ¼-in. diameter; knife or razor blade; narrow ribbons, yarn, or crepe paper for streamers.

procedure

1. Cut groove A along the length of the piece of cork to form the mouthpiece (Fig. 1).
2. Cut groove B around the middle of the mouthpiece (Fig. 1).
3. Slide the open end of balloon on the mouthpiece until it extends over the middle groove, B. Tie a string around balloon at B so the balloon cannot slip off (Fig. 2).
4. Tie streamers on neck of balloon at C (Fig. 2).
5. To operate comet, blow into groove A and fill balloon with air. Press finger down on groove in neck of balloon to prevent air from escaping. Aim balloon upward and release. It will fly into the air with the streamers trailing as a tail (Fig. 3).

average time required

30 minutes. The leader should cut and prepare corks for the participant who is in kindergarten or under six years of age. A short, 1-in. length of plastic tubing with a ¼-in. diameter can be used instead of the cork.

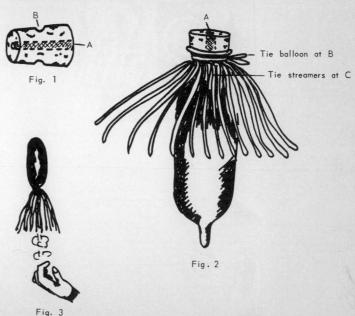

Fig. 1

Tie balloon at B

Tie streamers at C

Fig. 2

Fig. 3

handy sack rack

materials and tools

One large cereal box, a piece of construction paper, scissors, poster paints.

procedure

1. Cut off the top of the cereal box (Fig. 1).
2. Cover the cereal box with construction paper or paint it with poster paints (Fig. 2).

average time required

20 minutes

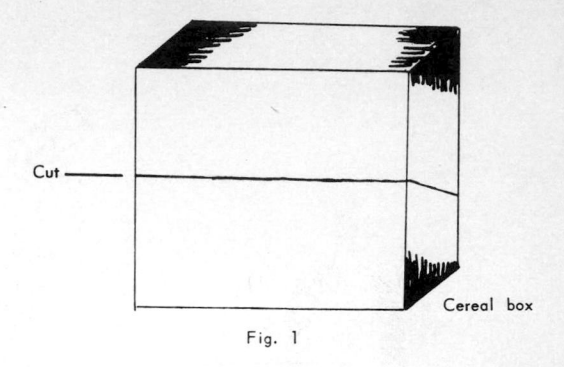

Cut

Cereal box

Fig. 1

Decorate

Fig. 2

hummer-drummer

materials and tools

One cardboard tube from a paper-towel roll, two rubber bands, some waxed paper, scissors, adhesive tape.

procedure

1. Cut a hole 3 in. long and 1 in. wide in the tube, 3 to 4 in. from one end.
2. Place a 6-in. piece of waxed paper around the tube so that the hole is covered.
3. Make sure the waxed paper is rolled firmly around the tube and then scotch-tape or use rubber bands to hold the edges of the paper down to the roll.
4. Cut a round piece of waxed paper and fold it over the end of the tube that is nearest to the side hole. Place a rubber band around the paper that is folded over the tube end or secure it with adhesive tape.
5. Wrap some adhesive tape around the open end of the tube. Place mouth to open end of tube and hum into the tube. The vibration is magnified by the waxed paper over the holes in the tube. To make a drumming noise, tap lightly with your fingers against the side hole or the end hole while humming through the instrument.

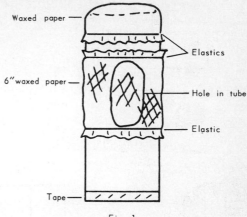

Fig. 1

milk-carton house or windmill

materials and tools

One-quart milk carton, glue, colored construction paper, scissors, crayons, paint, pin, knife or scraper, magazines.

procedure

1. Scrape off wax coat from carton at points where you will glue cover paper.
2. Place container on a sheet of construction paper and fold paper to fit carton. One sheet should completely cover the carton. Glue the paper securely to the carton.
3. Cut out a piece of construction paper for roof and glue to top (Figs. 1 and 3).
4. Decorate carton with paint, crayons, or cutouts from magazines to resemble a house or windmill (Figs. 2 and 3).
5. To make the windmill wheel, cut out a 5-in. square of construction paper; then use the techniques described in the project "Pinwheel," described in Part One.
6. Pin the wheel to the top of the carton (Fig. 2).

average time required

60 minutes

Fig. 1

Fig. 2

Fig. 3

paper-bag hats

materials and tools

Paper grocery bag large enough to fit the head of the child, crayons or paint.

procedure

1. Lay the paper bag flat and draw the desired shape on it.
2. Cut out the hat and decorate it with crayons or paint. Ideas for shapes are given in the illustrations (Figs. 1, 2, 3, and 4).
3. If you desire a hat with a lid or a bill, use the A part of the bag (Fig. 1).

average time required

30 minutes

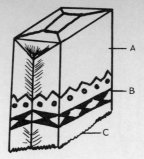

Fig. 1

Fig. 2

Fig. 3

Fig. 4

paper-bag halloween mask

materials and tools

Paper grocery bag large enough to fit over the head, crayons or dry felt ink marker, colored paper, glue, yarn, rope, or ribbon for hair.

procedure

1. Place the paper bag over the child's head and mark with a pencil (do not use a knife, nail, or sharp object to do this) the position of the eyes, nose, and mouth (Fig. 1).
2. Draw the face on the mask where the marks are, using a design of your choice. For safety make the eye holes large (Fig. 2).
3. Cut out the spaces for eyes, nose, and mouth. Using colored paper, crayons, or ink, make the face and ears. Hair and eyelashes may be painted on or made from yarn, rope, paper, or ribbon (Figs. 2, 3, and 4).
4. Put bag on head and tie ribbon or string around neck to keep the bag in the proper position (Fig. 4).

average time required

20 to 30 minutes. Variations such as a cat mask can be made by using straws from a broom for whiskers.

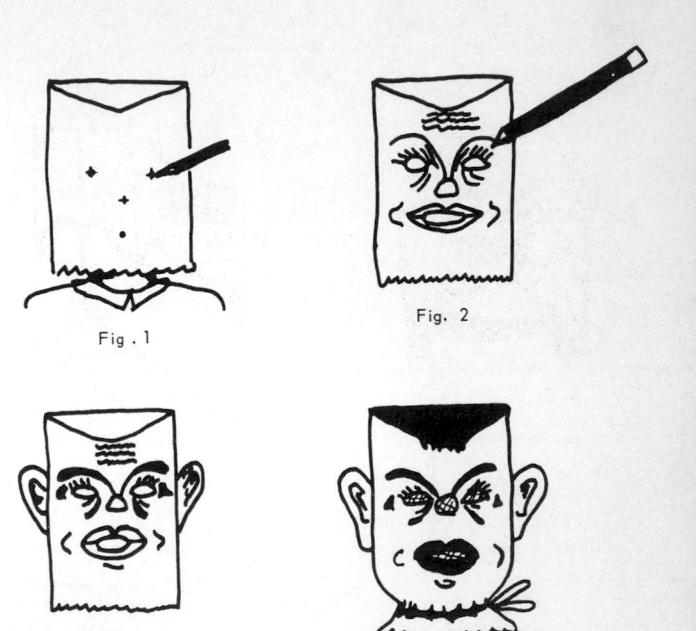

Fig. 1

Fig. 2

Fig. 3

Fig. 4

paper candy basket

materials and tools

One sheet of colored construction paper, scissors, stapler.

procedure

1. Cut the paper so that it is square; then fold it in half (Fig. 1).
2. Fold it in half again, bottom to top (Fig. 2).
3. Fold again to make a triangle (Fig. 3).
4. Trim the open edges at the top to the shape desired and make notches or lace cuts on the side edges only. Do not make the lace cuts too deep (Fig. 4).
5. Open the paper and you have an eight-cornered lacy figure (Fig. 5).
6. Bring opposite center folds A and B together and staple so that the basket has two pockets (Fig. 6).
7. Add the handle to the open pockets by stapling a strip of paper to the top of the basket from C to D (Fig. 7).

average time required

20 minutes

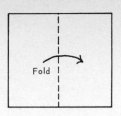

Fig. 1

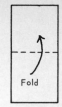

Fig. 2

Fig. 3

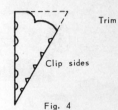

Fig. 4

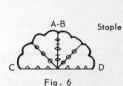

Fig. 5

Fig. 6

Fig. 7

paper-plate batik

materials and tools

One sheet of white paper, scissors, pencil, wax crayons, poster paint or water colors, a paper plate.

procedure

1. Draw a circle on the white sheet of paper the same size as the bottom of the plate. Cut it out. Fold it in half three times to form a cone (Figs. 1, 2, and 3).
2. On the folded sides cut a simple design (Fig. 3).
3. Trace the design on the plate. Color the design with brightly colored crayons (green, blue, orange, red, and yellow).
4. Using poster paint or water colors, paint the entire plate black or any deep or dark color. The paint is repelled by the crayon and will adhere only to the rest of the paper plate, making the design stand out.
5. Make slits in the rim of the plate and fasten a ribbon to hang the plate.

average time required

45 minutes. Suggestion—Use the technique described above and batik a picture or design upon a regular sheet of paper. Frame the picture and hang upon the wall.

34

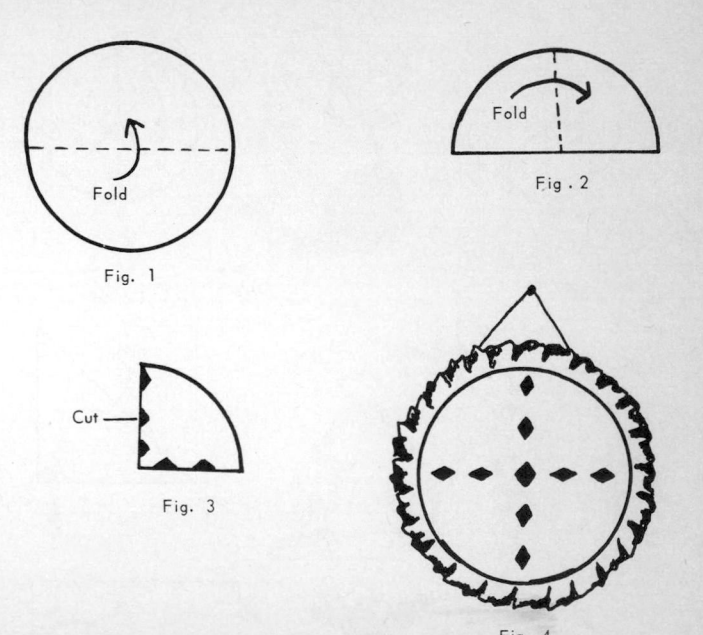

Fold

Fig. 1

Fold

Fig. 2

Cut

Fig. 3

Fig. 4

paper-plate mask

Fig. 1

materials and tools

Paper plate, paints, string, yarn, light cardboard.

procedure

1. Paint a face on the bottom of the plate.
2. Punch two string holes in the side of the plate.
3. Cut spaces for eyes, nose, and mouth. For safety make the eye holes large. For added attraction cut the edges to match the face pattern and add yarn for hair. To add humor to the mask, glue on a big nose cut from lightweight cardboard (Fig. 1).
4. Place string through the two holes in the paper plate. Place the mask over the face (Fig. 2).

average time required

30 minutes

Fig. 2

paper-plate note or letter holder

materials and tools

Two paper plates, colored yarn, crayons, paints, felt ink marker, paper punch or sharp nail, bobby pin.

procedure

1. Cut one of the paper plates in half. The other remains whole (Figs. 1 and 2).
2. Place half plate on the whole plate and punch holes through both plates. Be sure that the top sides of the plates are facing each other. The holes should be made big enough to thread yarn through both plates. If you do not have a paper punch, a pencil or a sharp nail will work (Fig. 3).
3. With the colored yarn, stitch the two plates together. A bobby pin may be used to push the yarn through the plates (Fig. 4).
4. Designs may be painted or drawn on the holder. Cutout pictures or pieces of colored paper can also be used to decorate the note holder. If you desire to batik the design, refer to "Paper-Plate Batik."
5. Punch a hole at the top of the holder and with a 6-in. length of yarn make a loop for hanging the holder on the wall (Fig. 5).

average time required

45 minutes. Six-year-old children and younger can punch holes with a nail. If a paper punch is used, the leader will have to do the punching or have some of the stronger boys do the job.

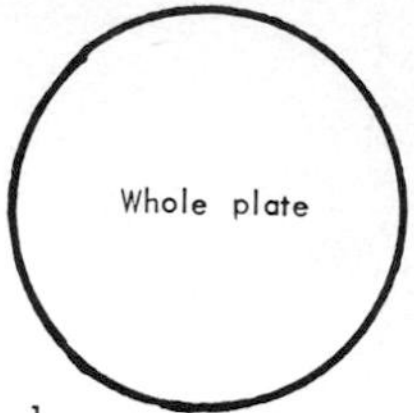

Fig. 1 — Whole plate

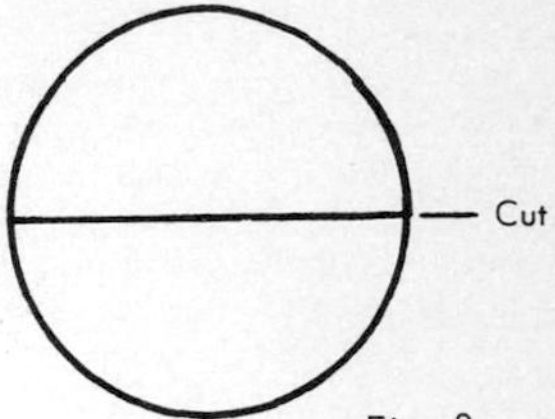

Fig. 2 — Cut

Fig. 3 — Punch holes

Fig. 4 — Stitch

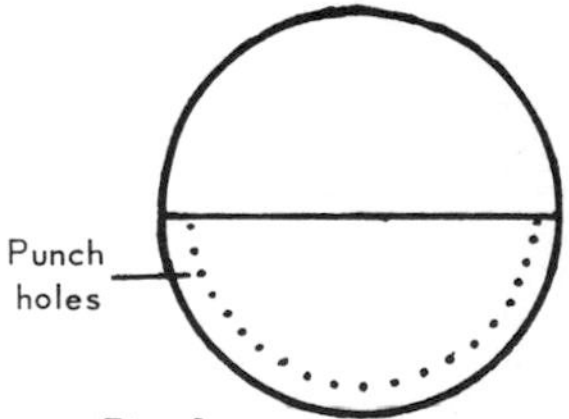

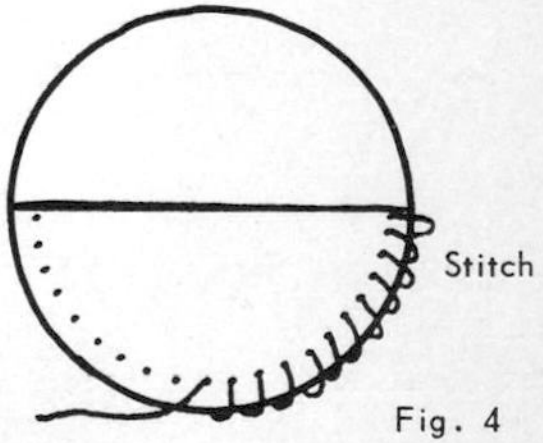

Fig. 5

peanut finger puppets

Figs. 1 — 5

materials and tools

Peanut shells, ink.

procedure

1. Break the peanut shells in half to form a thimble. Make one for each finger.
2. Put a face on each shell with ink (Figs. 1 to 5).
3. Place a shell face on each finger and make conversation with the puppets (Fig. 6).

average time required

30 minutes

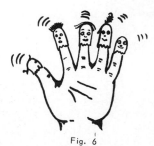

Fig. 6

pincushion

materials and tools

Jar ring and lid, cloth material, old nylon hose or handful of cotton, enamel paint (optional), pinking shears.

procedure

1. Paint lid and ring (Fig. 1).
2. Draw a 6-in. circle and a 7-in. circle on material and cut them out with pinking shears (Fig. 2).
3. Place the 6-in. circle of cloth in the ring (Fig. 3).
4. Place the cotton wad or nylon inside ring (Fig. 3).
5. Place the 7-in. circle of cloth on bottom, next to stuffing (Fig. 4).
6. Place the painted lid next to the 7-in. circle of cloth and push it up into ring to form pin cushion (Fig. 4).

average time required

35 minutes

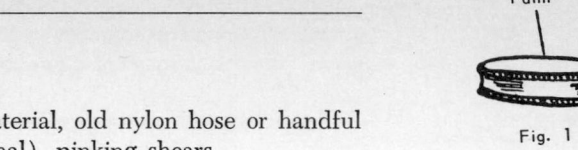

Paint

Fig. 1

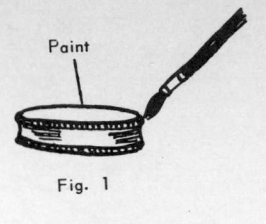

Fig. 2

Ring

Cotton

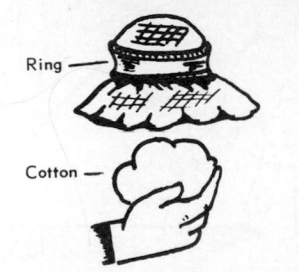

Fig. 3

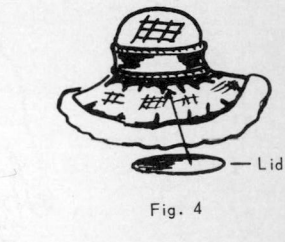

Lid

Fig. 4

Pincushion

pinwheel

materials and tools

One piece of construction paper, scissors, one straight pin, two beads or two small pieces of cardboard, one small stick or strip of board, pencil, ruler, hammer, any coloring medium desired.

procedure

1. Draw a 5- to 6½-in. square on the construction paper and cut it out. Make a circle 1 in. in diameter in the center of this square. Draw a straight or curving line from each corner of the square to the circle in the center. Cut along each line to the center circle. Decorate the pinwheel if desired (Fig. 1).
2. Place a small bead or a small piece of cardboard on the pin (Fig. 2).
3. Fold each corner (marked A, B, C, and D) into the center so that they lie on the circle with their ends overlapping about ¼ in. Stick the pin through the folded ends and the center of the square (Fig. 3).
4. Place another small bead or small piece of cardboard on the end of the pin and proceed to hammer or punch it carefully into the piece of wood (Fig. 4).

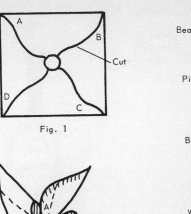

Fig. 1

Fig. 3

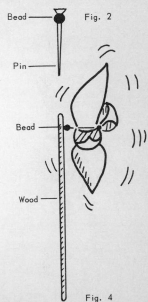

Fig. 2

Fig. 4

plastic-spoon dolls

materials and tools

Plastic spoons, colored ink, yarn, cloth scraps if you wish to dress the doll.

procedure

1. Paint features of doll on rounded side of the spoon. Glue on yarn for hair (Fig. 1).
2. Paint on clothes or use cloth to make them (Figs. 2 and 3).

average time required

15 minutes. The spoon doll can also be used as a book marker. Refer to "Wooden-Spoon Book Marker" in Part One.

Fig. 1

Fig. 2

Fig. 3

40

potato stencil

materials and tools

A potato, sheet of paper, ink or poster paint, knife, pencil.

procedure

1. Cut the potato in half (Fig. 1).
2. Using a soft pencil, draw or trace a design on the flat part of the potato (Fig. 2).
3. Cut away the potato from the design so that the design itself is raised above the rest of the potato at least ¼ in.
4. To stencil, dip the design into coloring and then place it against a piece of paper, using steady, light, even pressure on the stencil. Remove and repeat the process until the desired design is developed (Fig. 4).

average time required

45 minutes

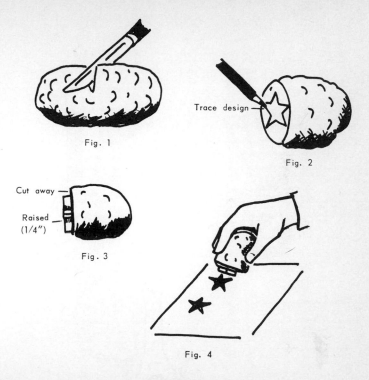

Fig. 1

Trace design

Fig. 2

Cut away

Raised (1/4")

Fig. 3

Fig. 4

sachet bag

materials and tools

Two round sheets of white paper about 5 in. in diameter, one piece of cotton, ribbon or colored yarn, sachet or perfume.

procedure

1. Place the two paper circles together and fold them three or four times, forming a cone. With sharp scissors cut designs along the folded edges. Unfold the cones, and you have two identical disks or doilies. (For folding and cutting techniques refer to the project "Paper-Plate Batik" in Part One.)
2. Place the cotton on top of one of the doilies. Saturate the cotton with sachet or perfume (Fig. 1).
3. Place the other paper disk, or doily, on top of the cotton. Be sure the cut designs are matching (Fig. 2).
4. Weave the ribbon in and out along the edge of the doilies, sewing them together. The weaving can be made to form an irregular design if desired (Fig. 3).
5. When completely sewed, tie the two ends of the ribbon together in a bow. If you wish to hang the bag in a closet, attach a ribbon to the side opposite the bow and tie it in a loop.
6. The sachet bag may be colored or decorated if desired.

average time required

20 minutes

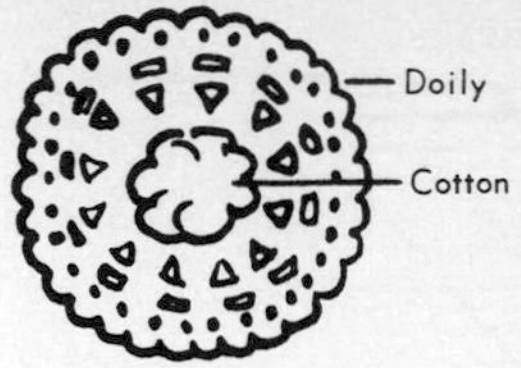

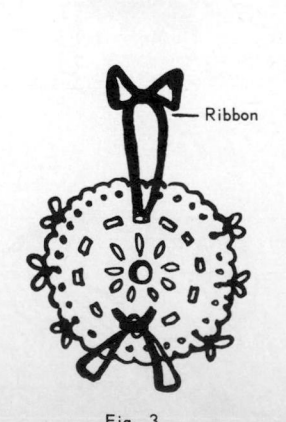

Fig. 1

Fig. 2

Fig. 3

sailboat

materials and tools

A block of wood about ½ to 1 in. thick by 4 in. wide by 10 in. long, tacks, string, paint, sandpaper.

procedure

1. Cut the wood in the shape of a boat (Fig. 1).
2. Sand the boat to remove the rough edges.
3. Fold the cardboard as in Fig. 2 and put a little slit at the tip for the string guide.
4. Tack the sail on the boat. Place the sail at about the middle of the boat or slightly forward of the center (Fig. 3).
5. Place a tack at front and rear of the boat and run a string from back to front, going over the sail in order to steady it.
6. Place tacks and string around boat edges to form a railing (Fig. 4).
7. Decorate or paint the boat as desired.

average time required

45 minutes

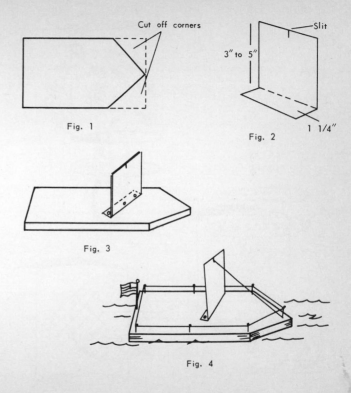

Cut off corners

Fig. 1

Slit

3" to 5"

1 1/4"

Fig. 2

Fig. 3

Fig. 4

sewing or scrap basket

materials and tools

A one- or two-gallon ice cream carton, wallpaper, heavy rug yarn, glue.

procedure

1. Glue wallpaper over all of the box and the top (Fig. 1).
2. Punch two holes in the opposite sides of the box ½ in. from the top. Also, punch two corresponding holes in the circular lid. These holes should be about ½ in. from the edge of the lid (Fig. 2).
3. Starting from inside the box, thread yarn through the side and lid holes and tie so yarn will become the handle (Fig. 3).

average time required

30 minutes

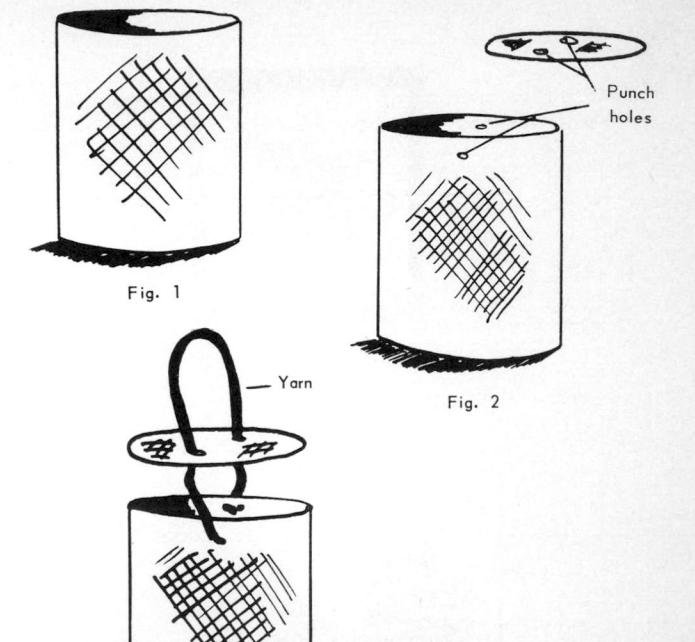

Fig. 1

Punch holes

Fig. 2

Yarn

Fig. 3

silhouette or profile picture

materials and tools

Large sheet of paper, a light that can be focused sharply, soft pencils, crayons.

procedure

1. Focus light on the wall (Fig. 1).
2. Place person between light and wall 6 to 12 in. from the wall. Place a piece of large white paper on the wall behind the person's head so that there is a clear shadow of his profile reflected on the paper (Fig. 1).
3. Trace the silhouette of the profile (Fig. 1).
4. Color the profile, or cut it out and place on a contrasting colored background (Fig. 2).

average time required

20 minutes

Flashlight

White paper

Shadow

Fig. 1

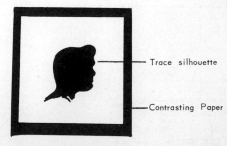

Trace silhouette

Contrasting Paper

Fig. 2

single-line checkerboard

materials and tools

Cardboard, checkers or buttons.

procedure

1. Cut out from the cardboard a checkerboard 15 by 5 in. (Fig. 1).
2. Start at one end of the board and place marks directly down its center at 1½-in. intervals (Fig. 1).
3. Place a checker over each marked interval and draw a circle around it. Number the marks from 1 to 9 (Fig. 2).
4. Game rules—place checkers of one color on spaces 1, 2, 3, 4, and checkers of the other color on spaces 6, 7, 8, 9. Determine which player will make the first move. Players take turns. Players may move one space or jump over one or more checkers as desired to an open space. The player cannot jump over an open space. The object of the game is to get all your checkers to the other end of the board before your opponent does. Space 5 must not be occupied by the winner.

average time required

30 minutes. This is a simple game to make, and an easy game to understand and to play. All age levels from 5 to 12 can enjoy this game. The higher age levels will enjoy making their board from wood and carving their own checkers. The board can be decorated, stained, and polished by the older participants.

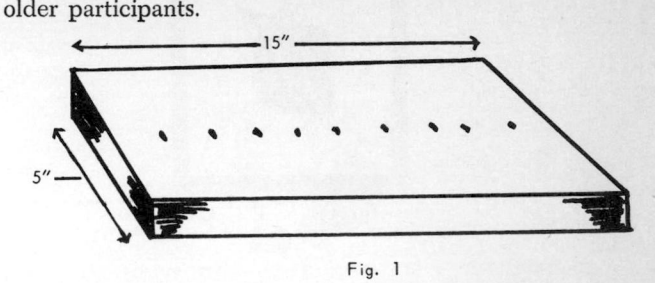

Fig. 1

Fig. 2

sound magnifier

materials and tools

Large nail, piece of string 28 in. long.

procedure

1. Tie nail tightly in the center of the piece of string (Fig. 1). With fingers, hold string ends in ears and then by moving the head sideways or forward and back, let the swinging nail strike a metal object (Fig. 2). The sound is greatly magnified. If a nail is not available, use a spoon. If no metal object is available, have someone flip the swinging nail with a fingernail.

average time required

10 minutes. This is a good project when studying the operation of a telephone. It demonstrates how sound vibrations travel along a wire or string.

Fig. 1

Fig. 2

sponge stenciling

materials and tools

A piece of sponge—any type, poster paint, wrapping paper.

procedure

1. Place the paper to be stenciled on a flat surface. First dip a section of the sponge in the poster paint and then press or daub it lightly against the paper. Keep pressing paint on the paper and move the sponge across the paper to form a design (Fig. 1).
2. If you want more than one color in the design, use another piece of sponge or re-use the first portion after cleaning it.
3. If you want to make a particular design (such as a diamond), cut the sponge into the required shape with a sharp knife, razor blade, or pair of scissors, and dot or daub on the paper as previously described. When making a stencil with a particular shape it is usually best to cut the sponge so that the design is raised above the original block of sponge (Fig. 2).
4. Success in the stenciling depends upon the ability to daub the sponge with the same amount of pressure each time and to keep the design straight.
5. Use the paper as gift wrapping or as fancy designs or as wallpaper. Use permanent ink or wall paint when making wallpaper.

Fig. 1

Raised design

Sponge

Fig. 2

48

stand-up double animals

materials and tools

Stiff white paper, pencil, crayons, thin paper or tracing paper for developing patterns.

procedure

1. Draw the figure of a dog on a piece of thin paper. In Fig. 1 notice how one of the hind legs of the dog is dotted in. This is to show the other half of the pattern.
2. Fold the paper on the center dotted line. Hold or place the folded paper against a bright window and trace the pattern with the dotted leg on the other side of the folded piece of paper. Be sure, when tracing the hind legs, to trace the dotted leg on one side and the completely filled in leg on the other side (Fig. 2).
3. Cut out the pattern and trace it on a piece of stiff white paper (Fig. 2).
4. Cut the animal out. Do not cut out the dotted lines at the top of the dog as these are for folds (Fig. 2).
5. Fold on the dotted lines and then stand the dog up.
6. Use crayons to color the animal.
7. This method can be used to develop many other animals.

Fold

Fig. 1

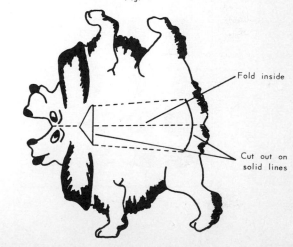

Fold inside

Cut out on solid lines

Fig. 2

49

average time required

40 minutes. The leader might need to prepare or help young participants make their own patterns. More mature participants (eight years and over) should be able to create their own.

string painting

materials and tools

Water colors, white paper, string, water.

procedure

1. Wet paper thoroughly on both sides.
2. Sponge or wipe off excess water.
3. Place a drop of water in each water color cup to be used for the picture.
4. Wet the piece of string with water; then saturate short sections of the string with different colors. One or several colors may be used on the piece of string.
5. Make designs by moving string across the paper in circular or other motions. The type of design is left up to the participant. Creativeness should be encouraged.
6. Let the paper dry when completed (Fig. 1).

average time required

30 minutes. An alternate method of string painting may be used, employing the methods described above to prepare the string but not wetting the paper. Fold the paper in half and on one section place the string as desired. Leave an end of the string protruding from the folded paper. Close the paper over the string and place a book or hand on top of folded paper. Grasp the protruding end of string and quickly pull it out from between the pages (Fig. 3). The result is an abstract design (Fig. 4).

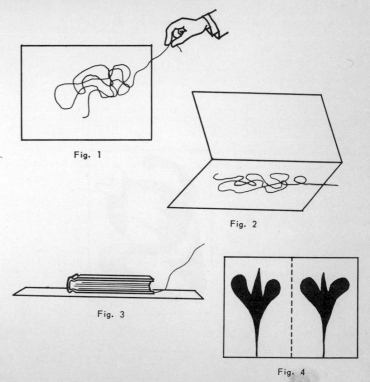

Fig. 1

Fig. 2

Fig. 3

Fig. 4

tell-me-about-it

materials and tools

A sheet of paper, pencil, crayons or water colors.

procedure

1. Using imagination and free-hand drawing, develop a design, shape, or figure on the paper.
2. Color with crayon and give the picture a title.
3. Have the participants tell what they think their picture represents.

average time required

Varies with age group and subjects attempted.

Fish asking for a handout

twine holder

materials and tools

One medium-sized, clean ice cream carton, paints and other decorations, such as sequins, glitter, buttons, feathers.

procedure

1. Paint a face on the carton and cut out the mouth for the string hole. Ears can be made from light cardboard and glued into place (Fig. 1).
2. Make a hat from the lid and decorate it with feathers, sequins, etc. (Fig. 2).

average time required

40 minutes. If the carton is oily, cover it with construction paper and then paint the face on the new material.

Fig. 1

Fig. 2

Side view

twirling colored disk

materials and tools

A piece of medium-heavy cardboard 3 by 3 in., a piece of string approximately 48 in. long, pencil compass or a pencil on a 4-in. piece of string, crayons.

procedure

1. From the cardboard cut a circle with a 3-in. diameter (Fig. 1).
2. Divide both sides of the disk into six sections; color them with many colors or paint each section with only one color (Fig. 1).
3. Make two holes about ½ in. apart in the center of the disk, thread string through the holes, and tie the ends of the string together (Fig. 2).
4. To operate the disk, place the thumbs between the loop at each end of the string and swing the disk in a circle to wind it (Fig. 3). When you spread or increase the distance between your hands, the disk spins as the string unwinds. When you relax the string or bring your hands closer together, the disk rewinds the string as it continues spinning (Fig. 4). Each time the hands are separated the direction of the spin changes. Watch the different color changes as the disk continues spinning.

average time required

30 minutes. A large button can be used instead of a cardboard disk. Buttons can be painted with a fast-drying enamel.

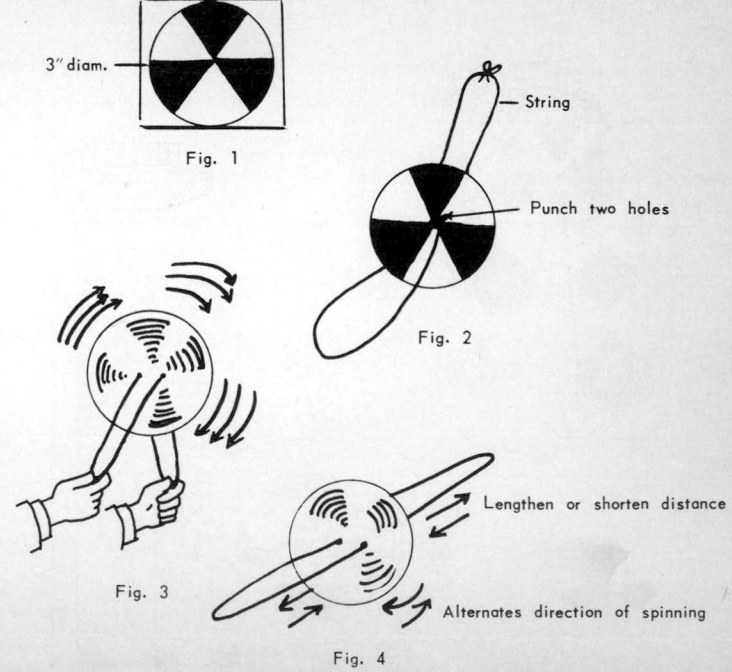

3″ diam.

Fig. 1

String

Punch two holes

Fig. 2

Fig. 3

Lengthen or shorten distance

Alternates direction of spinning

Fig. 4

the whirligig

materials and tools

A light piece of cardboard or sheet of heavy construction paper 7 by 2½ in., paper clips.

procedure

1. Draw design of the Whirligig on the heavy paper and cut it out. Cut along the line that divides flaps A and B (Fig. 1).
2. Fold on dotted lines. Be sure to fold flaps A and B in opposite directions (Figs. 2 and 3).
3. Fasten two or three paper clips to the folded edges of flaps C and D for weight and to secure the fold (Figs. 2 and 3).
4. To operate, toss the Whirligig into the air and it will whirl and flutter as it falls to the ground.

average time required

15 minutes if the pattern is provided. Older participants should make their own patterns. A gaily colored Whirligig is very effective and adds to the fun of making the project.

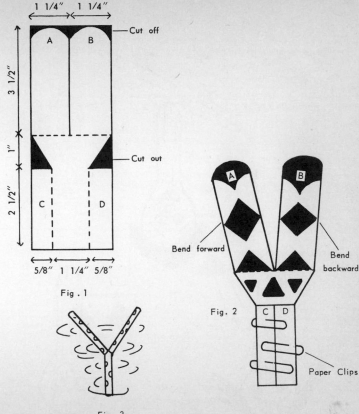

wooden-spoon book marker

materials and tools

Flat, wooden confectionary spoon, ink, colored yarn.

procedure

1. Draw a face on the wooden spoon with ink (Fig. 1).
2. Glue on the yarn for hair (Figs. 2 and 3).

average time required

15 minutes. If desired, use small buttons on the face—red button for the nose, etc.

Fig. 1

Fig. 2

Fig. 3

woolly lamb

Fig. 1

materials and tools

Large sheet of construction paper, colored art paper, crayons, cotton, glue, button.

procedure

1. Cut out drawing of lamb from white construction paper. The lamb should be made large enough to fill the large construction background sheet as in Fig. 1.
2. Color eye, ears, tongue, nose, feet, and ribbon around neck (Fig. 1).
3. Using colored art paper and glue construct a suitable background setting for the lamb. Grass makes a very effective background (Figs. 2 and 3).
4. Glue lamb on decorated construction paper.
5. Roll small pieces of cotton into tiny balls and glue close together, covering the entire lamb (Fig. 3).

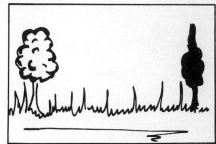

Fig. 2

average time required

60 minutes. Other animals can be made by this process. Fur can be used for animals, and feathers for birds. (Fur and feathers should be used only by older children.) If desired,

Fig. 3

57

buttons can be used for the nose and eye, and a narrow piece of brightly colored ribbon can be placed around the neck.

part two   second-grade ages

second-grade ages

Artwork Envelope **61**	Cutout Pictures— Cloth **69**	Paper-bag Bird **76**	Spool Top **85**
Balloon Figures **62**	Decorated Paper Clip **70**	Paper-bag Snowman **77**	Star Snowflake **86**
Christmas Chain **63**		Plastic-foam Man **78**	Stick Horse **87**
Color Twirler **64**	Fish Aquarium **71**	Record Flower Pot **79**	Stocking Puppets **88**
Cork Sailboat **65**	Flower Vase (Yarn) **72**	Rock Paperweights **80**	String Key Chain **89**
Cork Toys, Animals, or Figures **66**	Indian Headdress **73**	Sack Puppet **81**	Tin-can Stilts **90**
Crazy Racing Roller **67**	Indian Tepee **74**	Salt Beads **82**	Tin-can Telephone System **91**
Cutout Name Design **68**	Jet Plane **75**	Snip and Art **83**	Torn-paper Pictures **92**
		Spool Rack **84**	Tube Puppet **93**
			Yarn Basket **94**

artwork envelope

materials and tools

Heavy butcher or book cover paper 36 by 28 in., yarn, glue, paper punch, pencil, ruler, water colors.

procedure

1. Place heavy paper on a flat surface and with a pencil mark off the plan as shown in Fig. 1.
2. Cut off the 1-in. edges of section A and the corners of section C.
3. Fold in the 1-in. edges of section B and cover the top side of these edges with glue (Fig. 2).
4. Fold A flap over B flap and press down until the B edges are glued fast to the underside of the A flap (Figs. 2 and 3).
5. Decorate the front and back surfaces of the envelope with water colors or glue pictures selected from magazines.
6. With paper punch make holes ½ in. apart around the edges of the envelope. Weave in and out of the holes with yarn (Figs. 3 and 4).

average time required

40 minutes to make the envelope. The time for decoration is extra.

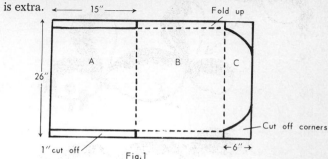

Fig. 1

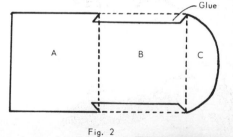

Fig. 2

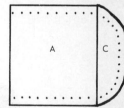

Fig. 3

Fig. 4

balloon figures

materials and tools

Various-size balloons (long ones preferred), poster paint or dry felt ink marker to paint faces or designs on the figures, string.

procedure

1. Decide upon the figure you wish to make. Blow up the balloon in sections, one section at a time. When the desired amount of air is in the section, twist it two or three times and hold it or tie it with string so it will not untwist while you are blowing up the other sections of the same balloon (Figs. 1 and 2).
2. When the animal or shape has been obtained, stretch the blowing end and tie it in a knot to prevent the air from escaping (Fig. 2).
3. To attach the legs make a two-piece-section balloon and wrap it around the sections of the balloon at the twisted area (Fig. 3).
4. Face and designs may be painted on with poster paint or dry felt ink marker.

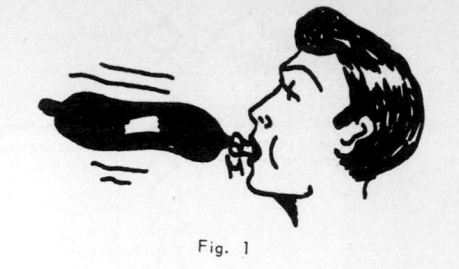

Fig. 1

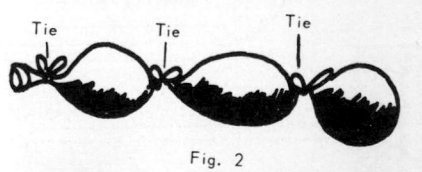

Tie   Tie   Tie

Fig. 2

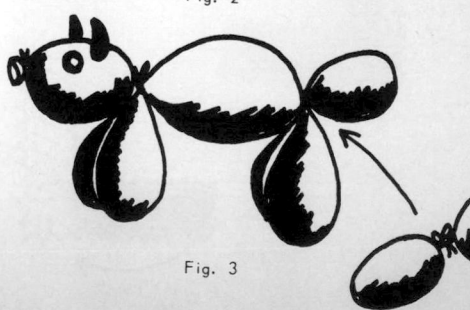

Fig. 3

62

christmas chain

materials and tools

Red and green colored crepe paper, glue, pinking shears, pencil.

procedure

1. Cut crepe paper into strips about 2 in. wide. (Make as wide or as narrow as desired).
2. Glue ends of two lengths of paper together at right angles to each other (Fig. 1).
3. Fold the two strips alternately one over the other until you have run out of paper (Figs. 1 and 2). Glue on other strips as needed to obtain the desired length of chain.
4. The finished product will be a stack of folds. Glue ends together when the desired length has been achieved. Holding both ends, extend or stretch out chain and fasten a string at top (Fig. 3). If desired, edges of crepe paper can be pulled out slightly with thumb and forefinger to give a ruffled appearance.

average time required

60 minutes

63

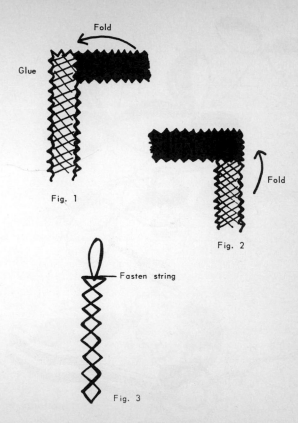

Fig. 1

Fig. 2

Fig. 3

Fold

Glue

Fold

Fasten string

color twirler

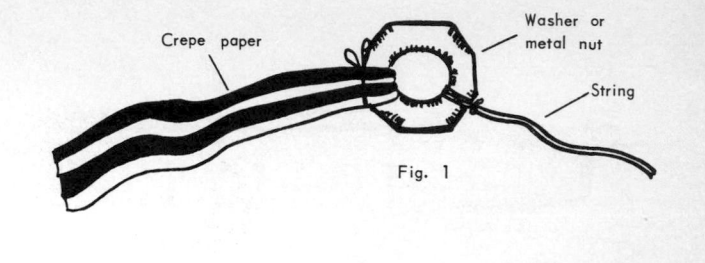

Fig. 1

materials and tools

Colored crepe paper, a piece of heavy string, medium-sized metal nut or heavy washer with a 1-in. diameter.

procedure

1. Cut the crepe paper into streamers 36 by 1 in.
2. Tie four differently colored streamers to the nut or washer (Fig. 1).
3. Tie a 15-in. cord to the washer (Fig. 1).
4. Hold the end of the cord in your hand and swing the colored twirler around your head in several directions. Develop many varied patterns with the twirler and the trailing streamers (Fig. 2).

average time required

15 minutes

Fig. 2

cork sailboat

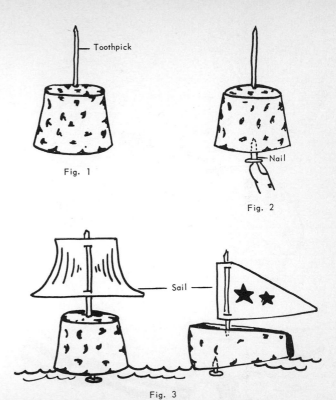

Fig. 1

Fig. 2

Fig. 3

materials and tools

Small cork, paper, shingle nail, toothpicks or straight pins, crayons, paints or dry felt ink marker.

procedure

1. Push toothpick into top of cork (Fig. 1).
2. Push nail into bottom of cork (Fig. 2).
3. Put paper sail on toothpick after decorating it with crayons, paints, etc.
4. It is now ready for launching (Fig. 3).

average time required

10 minutes. Variation—cut the cork in half lengthwise and place toothpick sail on flat surface. Push small nail into rounded surface or bottom of the boat. If the leader prepares the corks by cutting them in half, this boat project can be used in first grade; if not, this project is suitable for second- or third-grade participants.

cork toys, animals, or figures

materials and tools

Corks of assorted sizes, matches, nails, pipe cleaners, small buttons, colored paper, colored yarn, glue.

procedure

1. Use larger corks for body, smaller corks for head. By breaking off small bits of the matches, eyes, nose, and mouth can be stuck on the cork face.
2. To facilitate the insertion of matches, a sharp instrument such as a nail should be used to punch the required holes in the corks. Nails with large heads, or pipe cleaners (bent at ends), can be used for legs.

average time required

30 minutes. Buttons, sequins, or colored paper can be used for making faces, paper for animals' heads, and paper or string for tails. Pipe cleaners may be substituted for matches in making arms and legs. (Use only burned matches.) If the participants are interested, they can compete to see who can make the most objects from his supply of corks.

Fig. 1

Fig. 2

Fig. 3

Pipe cleaner

Fig. 4

crazy racing roller

materials and tools

Colored paper, paste, small marble.

procedure

1. Trace design on colored paper and cut it out (Fig. 1).
2. Fold flaps A and B toward the center strip.
3. To form the sides, place flaps A together and paste.
4. Insert the marble between the sides; then paste ends C and D together to form a bean-shaped roller with the marble on the inside (Fig. 2).
5. To operate the racer, release it on an inclined flat surface and it will roll down end over end with an erratic motion. Race the rollers against each other (Fig. 3).

average time required

20 minutes. When roller is used in a racing game, it can be adapted to higher age levels. When using larger marbles, adjust the size of the paper pattern.

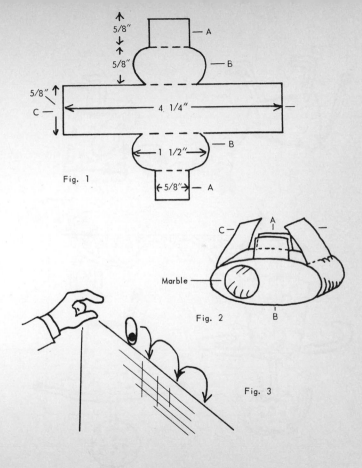

67

cutout name design

materials and tools

One piece of colored or plain paper, scissors, pencil.

procedure

1. Fold the paper lengthwise through the middle.
2. On the outside and along the folded edge write your name with double lines.
3. Cut out your name along the folded lines and when paper is unfolded you will have a beautiful design. Shade in background of design with crayons.

average time required

30 minutes

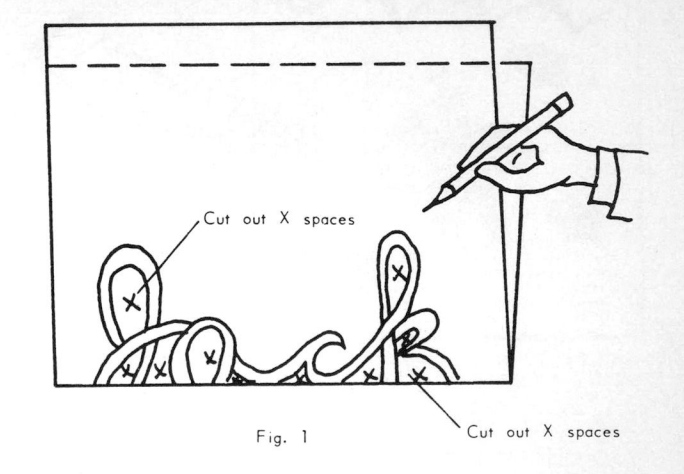

Cut out X spaces

Cut out X spaces

Fig. 1

cutout pictures–cloth

materials and tools

Colored paper, glue, scraps of cloth, scissors.

procedure

1. Cut out the desired shapes or designs from the material scraps and paste them on a piece of colored paper. A border can also be made (Figs. 1 and 2).

average time required

60 minutes. Variations can be made by substituting cutouts from magazines for cloth material. Other media that can be used to supplement the pictures are colored chalk, wallpaper, water colors, yarn, water paint.

Fig. 1

Fig. 2

decorated paper clip

materials and tools

One-half ping-pong ball or small ball of plastic foam insulation, water colors, small piece of cotton, spring-type clothespin, glue.

procedure

1. Glue the half ping-pong ball to the front end of the clothespin.
2. Make two ears and a nose out of cotton and glue to ball. Paint on eyes and mouth. Make tail of cotton and glue on end of clothespin opposite ping-pong ball.

average time required

20 minutes

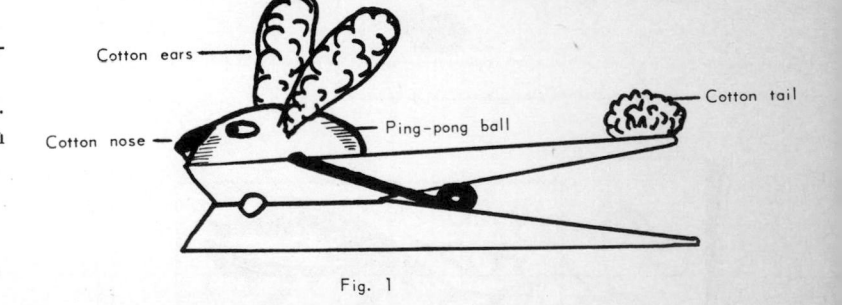

Cotton ears

Cotton tail

Cotton nose

Ping-pong ball

Fig. 1

fish aquarium

materials and tools

Saran Wrap, Handi-Wrap, or any transparent wrap paper, an electric iron, white or colored paper, scissors, crayons, green leaves (real or paper), two newspapers.

procedure

1. Make fish out of white or colored paper. If white is used, color the fish.
2. Place fish and leaves on lower half of wrap paper (Fig. 1).
3. Bring upper half of wrap paper down on top of fish and leaves (Figs. 1 and 2).
4. Place folded picture on a newspaper and before pressing, cover with a folded piece of newspaper. Press with moderately hot iron until wrap paper melts slightly or sticks together. This process should only take a few minutes. Care should be taken not to burn paper (Fig. 3).
5. To display in room, glue a frame of dark colored construction paper around the edges of the picture and hang in window with a piece of Scotch tape (Fig. 4).

40 minutes

Fig. 1

Fig. 2

Fig. 3

Fig. 4

flower vase (yarn)

materials and tools

Bottle (any shape) or a tin can, yarn, glue, needle, thread, beads.

procedure

1. Cover a section of the bottle with glue (Fig. 1).
2. Wrap yarn around outside of bottle, adding more glue and continuing until the bottle is completely covered (Fig. 2).
3. To decorate, glue or sew on buttons or yarn patterns as desired (Fig. 3).

average time required

45 minutes

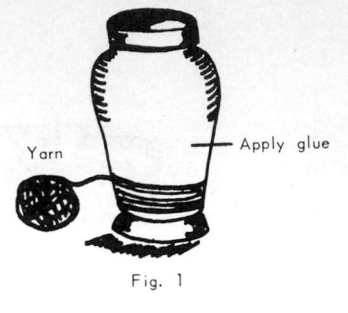

Yarn — Apply glue

Fig. 1

Fig. 2

Design

Fig. 3

indian headdress

Fig. 1

materials and tools

Newspaper or cardboard, stapler, turkey or chicken feathers.

procedure

1. Fold the newspaper or cut cardboard into a band about 1½ in. wide (Fig. 1).
2. Place the band around the head and mark the band for size. Make band 1 in. larger than head size for overlapping and fastening ends together. Before fastening (stapling or sewing) ends together, decorate band as desired (Fig. 2).
3. Staple the feathers to a small square of cardboard. Staple or glue the feathers to the back of the headband (Figs. 3 and 4).

average time required

30 minutes. Feathers may be dyed with any good cloth dye by placing them in a hot dye solution to remove the oil and allow the dye to enter the feathers.

Fig. 2

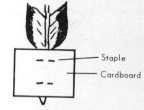

Fig. 3

Staple

Cardboard

Staple or glue

Fig. 4

indian tepee

materials and tools

A sheet of colored paper, four slender wooden sticks, Scotch tape, piece of string, crayons.

procedure

1. On a sheet of colored construction paper draw a 10-in. circle. Cut out the circle and then cut it in half.
2. Draw tent design on colored paper and decorate with Indian designs (Figs. 1 and 4).
3. Cut four sticks into 6 in. lengths. Hold them together about 1 in. from the top and tie with string. Spread apart at the top and bottom (Fig. 2).
4. Form tepee into a cone and tape the edges on the inside (Fig. 3).
5. Insert the sticks and spread them evenly around the inside of the tepee and fasten with tape (Fig. 4).
6. To make the door, cut a circular hole in front of tent. Make a circular flap and with tape placed inside so that it will not show, fasten the door flap in place (Figs. 3 and 4).

average time required

45 minutes

74

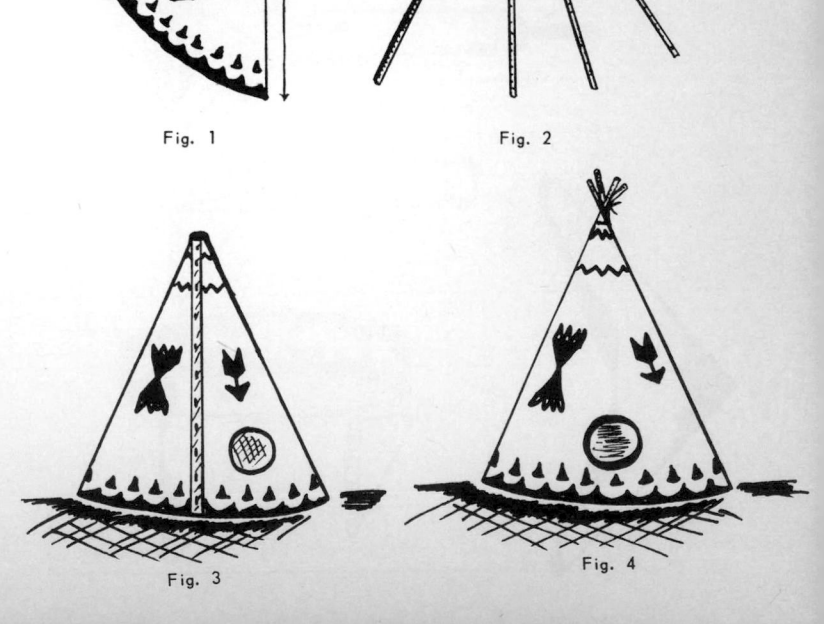

Fig. 1

Fig. 2

Fig. 3

Fig. 4

jet plane

materials and tools

A solid, two-prong clothespin, golf tee, crayons, cardboard, glue, pencil, scissors.

procedure

1. Cut the required tail sections from cardboard (Figs. 1 and 2).
2. Cut off one of the blades of the clothespin and glue it to the top side blade as shown in Fig. 4.
3. Cut a slit ½ in. long in the end of the blade of the clothespin and slide the top section (Fig. 2) into the slit as in Fig. 4.
4. Glue the bottom section (Fig. 1) to the underside of the blade of the clothespin (Fig. 5).
5. Glue the golf tee to the head of the clothespin (Fig. 5).
6. Cut the wings from cardboard as shown in Fig. 3. Glue the wings to the undersection of tail blade as in Fig. 6. Use crayons to decorate jet (Fig. 6).

average time required

40 minutes

75

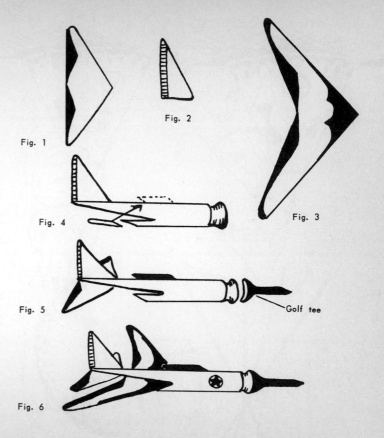

Fig. 1
Fig. 2
Fig. 3
Fig. 4
Fig. 5 — Golf tee
Fig. 6

paper-bag bird

materials and tools

Paper bag, newspaper, string, a few sheets of colored paper, glue, scissors, pencil, ruler.

procedure

1. Stuff the bag with newspaper and tie upper third securely with string. This will be the head (Fig. 1).
2. Stuff the lower part of the paper bag with more newspaper and tie securely with string. This is the body and should be larger than the head (Fig. 2).
3. Cut out the bird's face from the piece of colored paper. Cut out two round circles for the bird's eyes. Glue the eyes to the bird's head as shown in Fig. 3.
4. Glue face on the head of the bird (Fig. 4).
5. Cut two wings and a tail if you desire (Fig. 5).
6. Glue the wings and tail to the bird's body (Fig. 6).

average time required

40 minutes

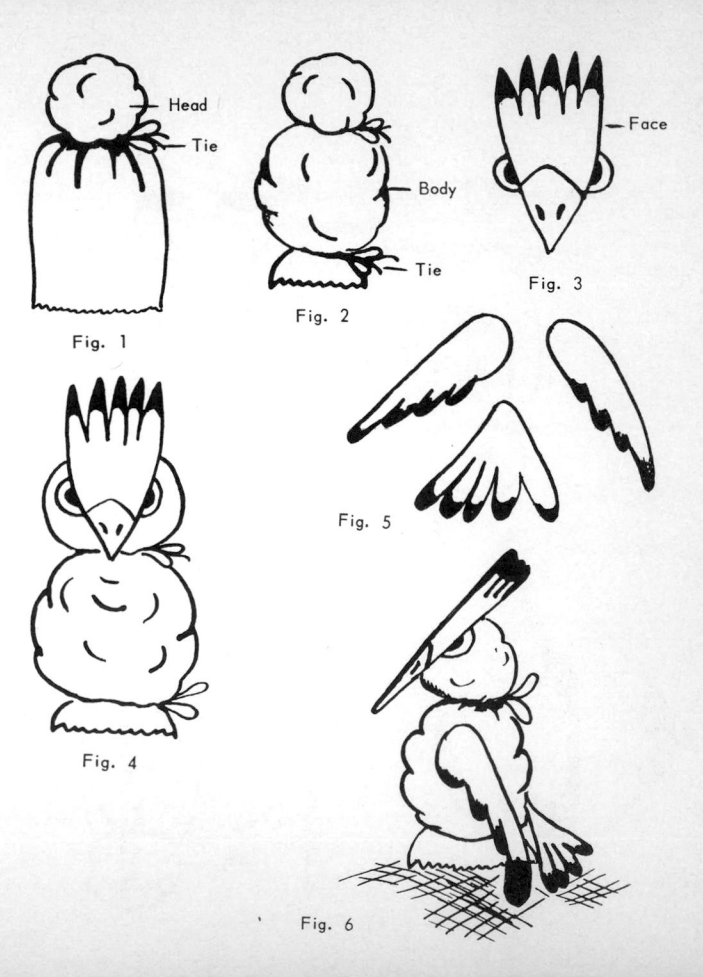

Fig. 1

Fig. 2

Fig. 3

Fig. 4

Fig. 5

Fig. 6

paper-bag snowman

materials and tools

A piece of cardboard 5 by 5 in., a white paper bag, crayons, string, newspaper.

procedure

1. Stuff the paper bag with torn newspaper and tie upper third with string. This will be the man's head (Fig. 1).
2. Stuff the lower part of the bag with paper until snowman has a large round body and tie securely (Fig. 2).
3. Draw snowman's features with black crayon—use buttons for eyes if desired.
4. From cardboard cut out two wide feet and sew or glue them in place (Fig. 3).

average time required

40 minutes. To make the figure look more like snow, place glue over paper bag and wrap a thin layer of cotton over it. Add features after cotton is securely glued to paper.

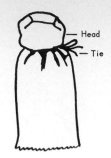

Fig. 1

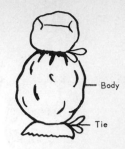

Fig. 2

Front

Side

Fig. 3

plastic-foam man

materials and tools

Small block of plastic foam or styrene, small ball of paper, piece of light cardboard, piece of white cloth, pen and ink, crayons, glue, string, common straight pins, sharp knife.

procedure

1. Make a head by tying the cloth around the paper ball (Fig. 1).
2. Mark the face on the cloth and color it with crayons or ink (Fig. 2).
3. Make the man's body from the block of foam. With a knife cut the body either round or square and about 2 by 3 in. (Fig. 3).
4. To fasten the man's head to his body, glue the white cloth material extending below the head to the top of the man's body (Fig. 2).
5. Draw the arms and other designs on the man's body, or glue or pin on cardboard cutouts (Fig. 5).
6. Cut out feet from a piece of cardboard and pin them to the bottom of the man's body (Figs. 4 and 5).

45 minutes

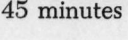

Fig. 1

Fig. 2

Fig. 3

Pin

Cardboard foot

Fig. 4

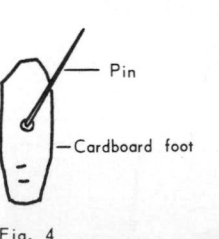

Fig. 5

record flower pot

Fig. 1

materials and tools

Old phonograph records (all sizes), tin can, oven, paint, gloves to handle hot records.

procedure

1. Place the phonograph records on a tin can and put in the oven, which has been preheated to about 350° (Fig. 1). The disks will soften quickly and must be watched carefully to prevent them from becoming overheated. As they heat they fold down and around the can, forming a vase shape (Fig. 2).
2. Leave folded disks on can and remove from oven; let cool and harden. Paint and decorate as desired (Fig. 3). To cool more quickly and retain the desired shape, run cool water over the molded record.

average time required

60 minutes. The leader should handle the oven and hot disks for young participants.

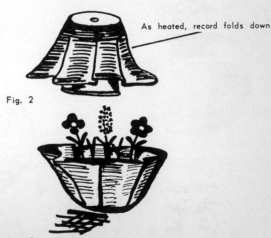

Fig. 2

Fig. 3

79

rock paperweights

Fig. 1

materials and tools

Rocks of different sizes and shapes, ink, enamel paints, or Magic Marker.

procedure

1. Study the rocks and select one that has a noticeable characteristic or a shape that resembles a figure or face (Fig. 1).
2. Wash and clean the rock and then color or decorate as desired (Fig. 2).

Fig. 2

average time required

30 minutes

sack puppet

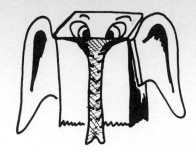

Fig. 1

materials and tools

Paper bag, colored paper, crayons.

procedure

1. Using colored paper, cut out ears, nose, and eyes.
2. Glue pieces in place on the sack. Decorate as desired (Fig. 1).
3. Place hand inside sack (as in Fig. 2) to move puppet.
4. Use imagination and develop different types of human or animal faces.

average time required

30 minutes

Fig. 2

salt beads

materials and tools

One-half cup flour, ¼ cup salt, ½ teaspoon sugar, ⅛ cup water, 2 drops food coloring, 1 drop of perfume, a piece of corrugated cardboard, toothpicks or pins.

procedure

1. Mix salt, sugar, and flour together in bowl.
2. Gradually add water with coloring and perfume to mixture. If mixture is too thin or sticky, work more flour and salt into dough until the right consistency is obtained.
3. Mold with fingers until you have a hard, but workable dough.
4. Measure the dough so the beads will be the same size. Make a long, even roll of dough and cut into even sections (Fig. 1).
5. Roll small pieces of dough in palm of hand until round, oval, or square, as desired (Fig. 2).
6. To make a hole in the bead, insert a toothpick or pin through its middle. Stick pin with the bead into a piece of cardboard to allow the bead to dry properly (Fig. 3). Allow sufficient time to dry. This usually takes about 48 hours.
7. When beads are dry, remove from pins and thread them on a string to form a necklace (Fig. 4).

82

average time required

30 minutes or more to make, plus additional time to string when dry. If you wish to make dough and preserve it for a short time, add a bit of glycerin and place it in a plastic bag. Adapt project to higher age levels by allowing participants to mix dough and make beads of different shapes and sizes.

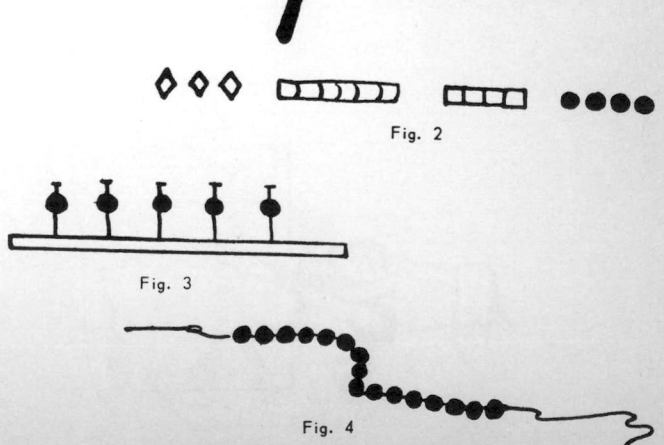

Fig. 1

Fig. 2

Fig. 3

Fig. 4

snip and art

materials and tools

One large sheet of paper (8 by 10 in.) of any color desired, scraps of colored paper, glue, scissors, crayons.

procedure

1. Cut out pieces from colored paper scraps and paste them onto the large back sheet, making any design or picture desired (Figs. 1 and 2).
2. For variation, parts of the picture can be completed with crayons or water colors (Fig. 2).

average time required

40 minutes

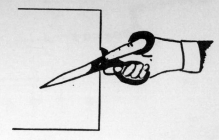

Fig. 1

Finish with crayons

Fig. 2

spool rack

materials and tools

Block of wood 13 in. long, 9 in. wide, and ½ to 1 in. thick, paint or stain, thumb tacks, ribbon or crepe paper, string or yarn, fourteen 2-in. finishing nails (small heads).

procedure

1. Sand wood block and paint or stain it. Let dry. Instead of painting it, you may prefer to glue on a picture from a magazine or cover the block with quilted plastic or some other suitable material.
2. Place nails evenly on board as shown in illustration. The top and bottom rows of nails are for small spools and the middle row is for big spools. Drive nails about ½ in. into wood.
3. With thumb tacks or glue fasten a crepe paper or ribbon ruffle around edge of board. Make a bow at top center of board.

average time required

45 minutes

Fig. 1

spool top

materials and tools

Wooden spool, piece of round wood for a peg, piece of string 4 ft. long, sharp knife or razor blade.

procedure

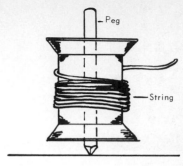

Fig. 1

1. With a knife shape the peg until it will slide into the spool and remain fast. The peg should extend ½ in. beyond the bottom of the spool and the end should be pointed. The top of the peg should extend 1 in. above the top of the spool (Fig. 1).
2. To operate the top, wind the string around the middle of the spool and, with the fingers of one hand, grasp the top of the peg and hold it in an upright position with the point resting solidly on a smooth surface. Pull the string sharply with the other hand and let the peg twist easily between your fingers. When the string has been withdrawn from the spool, release the top and let it spin by itself (Fig. 2).

Fig. 2

average time required

30 minutes

star snowflake

materials and tools

One square of paper any size desired, scissors.

procedure

1. Fold the corner A to B as in Fig. 1, forming Fig. 2.
2. Fold the corner C up and over D as in Fig. 2, forming Fig. 3.
3. Fold A edge in Fig. 3 up over C. Notice the fold divides the angles 1, 2, and 3 into three equal parts. Now fold flap D down and under, forming Fig. 4.
4. Cut a straight line from A to B if you want a star (Fig. 4).
5. To make a snowflake, fold the pattern (Fig. 4) on the dotted line D to form a cone (Fig. 5). Cut small pieces from edges AB and AC. Cut a jagged but rounding edge from B to C. Open pattern and you have a beautiful snowflake (Fig. 6).

average time required

15 minutes

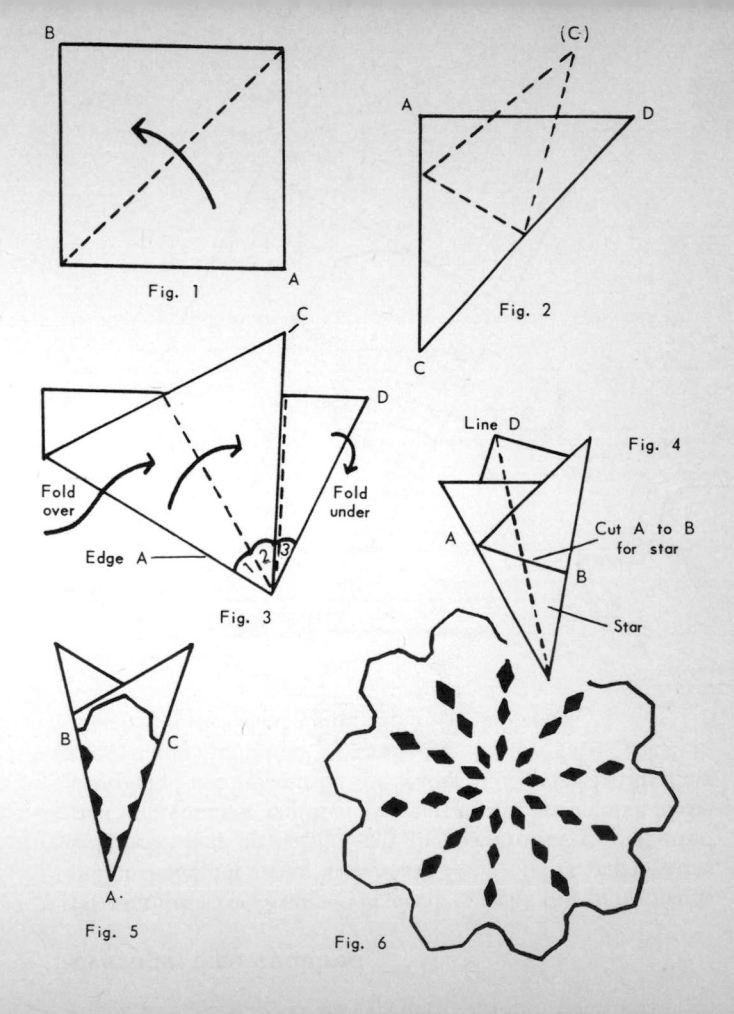

Fig. 1

Fig. 2

Fold over

Fold under

Edge A

Fig. 3

Line D

Fig. 4

A

Cut A to B for star

B

Star

Fig. 5

Fig. 6

86

stick horse

materials and tools

Heavy cardboard (piece from cardboard box), 8-in. pieces of yarn, 18-in. yarn or heavy twine, one stick (may vary in length and width), four tacks.

procedure

1. Fold cardboard in half. Draw a horse's head and part of its neck on one side of the cardboard. Unfold cardboard and cut out the horse's head and neck but do not cut on fold (Fig. 1).
2. Fold the cardboard again and trace the horse's head and neck on the uncut piece of cardboard. Cut out this second section but do not cut on fold. You now have the two sections of the head attached at the fold.
3. Insert the stick between the two heads and along the fold. Use tacks to hold the head and neck in place (Fig. 1).
4. Punch holes through the neck, below the stick. Insert several strands of yarn through the holes and tie to form the mane (Fig. 1).
5. Punch a hole in the mouth for reins. Use 18-in. yarn for reins (Fig. 2).

average time required

60 minutes. The leader will need to help the participants punch holes for mane and reins. Some of the participants will need help in cutting out the pattern. It is suggested that for younger children the cardboard heads should be completed beforehand by the leader. This would still allow the younger children to draw the horse's face, color it, attach the stick, and tie on the mane and reins.

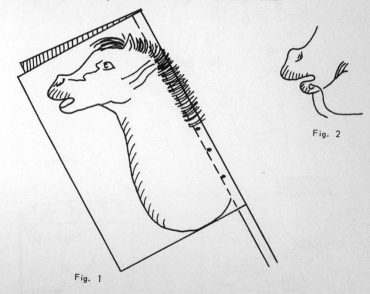

Fig. 2

Fig. 1

stocking puppets

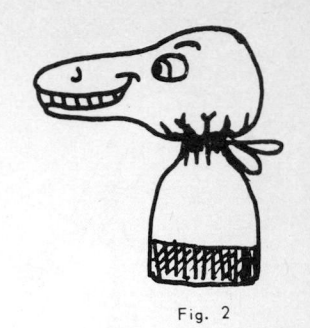

Fig. 1

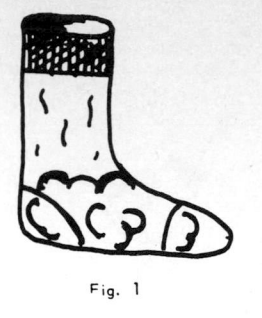

Fig. 2

materials and tools

One white anklet, piece of string 3 in. long, newspaper, crayons.

procedure

1. Tear newspaper into small pieces and stuff them into the stocking to form a head. The paper must be stuffed firmly and the sock stretched to acquire the needed shape. The head can be any shape desired (Figs. 1, 2, and 3).
2. Tie the string tightly around at the bottom of the head, leaving enough room for the index finger to fit through so that it can manipuate the head (Fig. 3).
3. Mark and color the features of the face with crayons. A hat or hair can be placed on the head, buttons sewed in place for eyes, etc. (Figs. 2 and 3).

Fig. 3

average time required

15 minutes

string key chain

Fig. 1

materials and tools

String, wooden peg or nail, key.

procedure

1. Take a piece of string three times the length of desired key chain. Double the string and tie the ends together. Put the untied, folded end of the string over the wooden peg or nail. Place the tied end over a chair corner or have someone hold it securely (Fig. 1).
2. Turn the peg, thereby twisting the string. Twist the string until it is quite tight.
3. Slip the string off the peg, holding both ends tightly so the string does not unwind. Slip the key over the string to the center, still making sure the string does not unwind (Fig. 2).
4. Double the twisted string by bringing the tied end to the folded end. Hold these two ends with one hand and the key with the other (Fig. 3). Now release the key, and the string will twist together with the appearance of a braid (Fig. 4).
5. Tie the open end together with another piece of string so the chain cannot unwind. (Fig. 4).

Fig. 2

Fig. 3

Fig. 4

89

tin-can stilts

materials and tools

Two tin cans of the same size, nail, hammer, 6 ft. of strong ¼-in. rope.

procedure

1. With the nail, punch two holes opposite each other, ½ in. down from the unopened end of each can (Fig. 1).
2. Cut the rope in half and thread the ends of one piece of the rope into the two holes of one can. Pull the ends to the inside of the can and tie them together securely (Fig. 1). Repeat with the other can.
3. To operate, place the cans about a foot apart on the ground. Take hold of each rope at its center with your hands and then place your feet on the cans between the ropes. Pull firmly on the rope to keep the cans in place while you are walking around (Fig. 2).

average time required

30 minutes

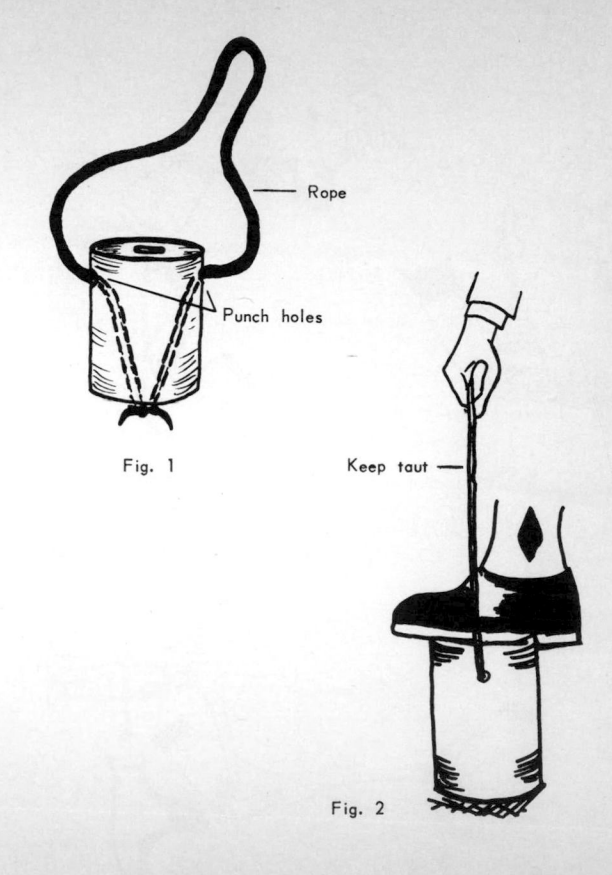

Rope

Punch holes

Fig. 1

Keep taut

Fig. 2

tin-can telephone system

materials and tools

Two tin cans (size 2½), nail, hammer, 20 to 50 ft. of string, two buttons.

procedure

1. With hammer and nail, punch a small hole through the top of each can (Fig. 1).
2. Thread the string through the hole in each can and tie a button to the end of each string to prevent it from slipping out of the can (Fig. 2).
3. Stretch the string tightly. One person places one can over his ear; the other talks into the second can.
4. Wax the string for better reception.

average time required

15 to 20 minutes

Fig. 1

Button

String

Fig. 2

Fig. 3

torn-paper pictures

materials and tools

Colored paper, glue, background paper 8½ by 10 in., any other decoration desired.

procedure

1. Tear colored paper as desired and glue to the background paper, forming a picture or design (Figs. 1, 2, and 3).
2. With pencil or crayon, add any decoration you wish.
3. To frame the picture, glue it onto a larger sheet of paper, leaving an even border (Fig. 3).

average time required

30 minutes

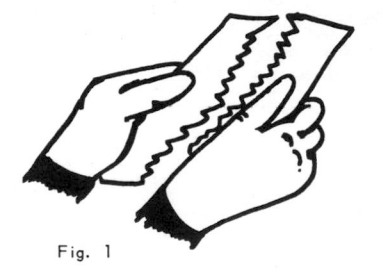

Scene

Fig. 2

Fig. 1

Background paper

Design

Fig. 3

tube puppet

materials and tools

A cereal box or small cardboard tube, yarn, crepe paper, crayons, paste, scissors, needle, thread, stapler, glue, printed cloth, buttons, masking tape, rickrack, old costume jewelry, feathers, beads, paper, and any other scraps with which to decorate your puppet.

procedure

1. Decide on what type of person or animal you wish your puppet to represent. Design the face with crayons or other media (Fig. 1).
2. Dress the puppet with collected materials, using your own ingenuity and imagination (Fig. 1).
3. The body can be made of cloth or crepe paper (Fig. 1).
4. Make a small tube of construction paper that fits snugly over your index finger. This tube is fastened to the inside wall of the puppet head by means of staples or glue. Insert your index finger in this tube to animate the head (Fig. 2).

average time required

40 minutes

93

Fig. 1

Fig. 2

yarn basket

materials and tools

Ball of yarn, cardboard or poster paper, picture from magazine, scissors, pencil, ruler.

procedure

1. Cut a 9½-in. circle from the cardboard (Fig. 1).
2. Around the outside edge of the cardboard circle, measure
   2 in. alternately with ½ in. Mark with pencil as you measure
   around the circle. You should have eleven 2-in. flaps (Fig.
   2).
3. Using a short string and pencil as a compass, draw a circle
   2 in. inside the 9½-in. cardboard circle. From the ½-in. marks
   draw two lines centerward and converging at the inside
   circle, forming a V. Cut out this V with scissors (Fig. 1).
4. Fold the flaps of the cardboard toward the center of the
   circle (Fig. 2).
5. Place yarn between two flaps and hold it securely; then
   begin to weave it in and out clockwise around the flaps.
   Soon you can release your hold on the end of the yarn and
   it will be held fast by the thread over it. Keep weaving
   until the yarn is within ¼ in. of the top (Fig. 2).
6. Cut yarn and tuck it securely beneath one of the sections.
   This will hold it and leave no stray end (Fig. 2).

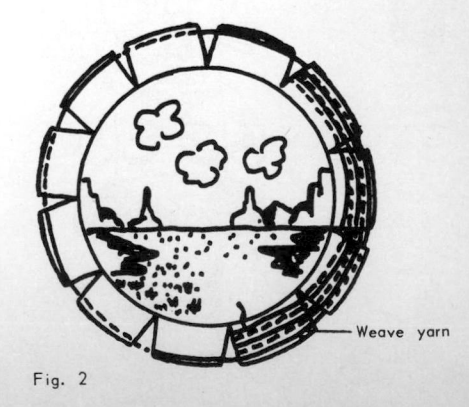

Cut out

1/2"

2"

Fig. 1

Weave yarn

Fig. 2

7. Paste a brightly colored picture in the inside of the basket or paint your own picture or design there (Fig. 2).

average time required

60 minutes. For variation, crepe paper or raffia may be used instead of yarn. Twist crepe paper for best results.

part three third-grade ages

third-grade ages

Aluminum-foil Picture	99	Crayon-Eraser Picture	107
Belt Weaving	101	Crepe-paper Basket	108
Bright-button Picture	102	Doll or Puppet Hat	110
Buttonhole Puzzle	103	Egg-carton Caterpillar	111
Buzzy Bee	104	Egg-cup Tulips	112
Colored-salt Picture	105	Glitter Vase	113
Cord Holder	106	Hobbyhorse	114
		Indian Rattle	115

Kite	116	Propelled Boat	124
Moving-shadow Figures	118	Ring Toss	125
Paper Beads	119	Spatter Painting	126
Parachute	120	Spool Knitting	127
Peanut Man	121	Stocking Hand Puppets	129
Plaster Picture Frame	122	Stuffed Rubber Doll	130
Powered Houseboat	123	Tambourine	131
		Willow Whistle	132

aluminum-foil picture

materials and tools

Smooth-type aluminum foil, a rubber-tipped bobby pin, dull pencil, masking tape, magazine.

procedure

1. Select a design and place it upon the shiny side of the foil. Hold it in place with masking tape.
2. Place the work on a magazine and trace with a pencil all the lines of the design (Fig. 1). Check the back side of the foil to see that all lines have been traced.
3. Remove the design and trace again over each line to deepen it. Do not press too hard to avoid cutting into the foil.
4. Turn the picture over so that the back side shows and re-trace the the lines just inside and near to the other lines, but not directly on them.
5. Keeping the back of the picture toward you, take the bobby pin and, using its rounded end or tip, carefully emboss the picture or push the design out so that the picture protrudes in front (Fig. 2).
6. Turn the picture face up on the hard surface of the table and, using the bobby pin, carefully smooth down the entire background. Use your finger to smooth down larger areas.
7. Frame or mount the picture as desired.

99

Shiny

Fig. 1

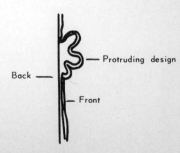

Protruding design

Back

Front

Fig. 2

average time required

90 minutes. Suggestions—use simple line drawings. Have the children select or draw their pictures before giving them materials. For durability, place the finished pictures on cardboard before framing. Disadvantages—the foil wrinkles and tears easily, and the picture flattens with too much pressure.

belt weaving

materials and tools

Three to five pieces of narrow plastic tubing about 4 in.
long, or drinking straws, colored yarn, 2½-in. wooden peg.

procedure

1. Use three, five, or more straws, according to the width of
   band or belt you wish to make. Thread the tubes with yarn
   long enough to fit around your waist and tie the exposed
   ends around the wooden peg. The tubes are your loom
   (Fig. 1).
2. Take a piece of yarn long enough for weaving and tie it
   at point B, on one side of the loom (Fig. 1).
3. Weave the yarn in and out of the tubes (Fig. 1). When
   you have completed several layers, slip them off the straws
   in the direction of point A.
4. Continue weaving and pushing off until the belt is the
   desired length. Secure by tying the end of the weaving
   yarn to one of the loom yarns.
5. Pull the ends of the loom strings from the tubes and tie
   them securely, forming a loop (Fig. 2).
6. To fasten the belt, place it around your waist and slide the
   peg through the loop (Fig. 3).

average time required

60 minutes

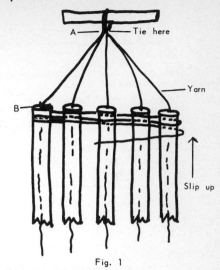

Fig. 1

Fig. 2

Fig. 3

bright-button picture

materials and tools

Colored buttons, thread, crayons, sheet of heavy white paper.

procedure

1. Draw the outline of a picture (Fig. 1).
2. Sew brightly colored buttons on the picture as desired (Fig. 2).
3. Color the background of the picture with crayons.

average time required

40 minutes. Instead of using crayons to develop the background, use glue and make it with rocks, leaves, grass, sand, twigs, and so forth.

Fig. 1

Yellow button

Red apple buttons

Fig. 2

buttonhole puzzle

materials and tools

One pencil 5 in. long or any wooden object the same length and size, piece of string.

procedure

1. Tie the ends of the string around the top of the pencil or peg so that the string forms a loop ½ in. shorter than the pencil or peg. When using a peg, bore a small hole at its top and run the string through to make the loop (Fig. 1).
2. Place the loop of string over a buttonhole on blouse or coat (Fig. 2).
3. Grasp the buttonhole and pull it and the cloth surrounding it through the string loop until the end of the peg will slip through the buttonhole (Fig. 3).
4. Slide the peg through the buttonhole and pull it to tighten string (Fig. 4).
5. To remove the peg, push the head or top of it back through the buttonhole (Fig. 5). Now spread the loop as wide as possible and reach through the loop and grasp the material; then pull it up through the loop (Figs. 3 and 5). Keep pushing the loop back and farther down on the material until the end of the peg can be removed from the buttonhole.

The object of this trick is to perform the first four steps without anyone seeing you, then ask someone to remove the peg without untying or breaking the string.

average time required

10 minutes

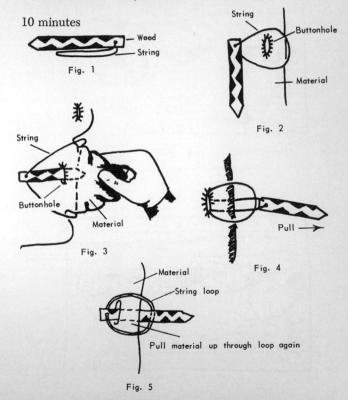

Fig. 1

Fig. 2

Fig. 3

Fig. 4

Fig. 5

buzzy bee

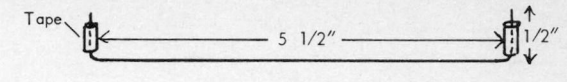

Fig. 1

materials and tools

A sheet of construction paper 4 by 6 in., piece of clothes hanger wire 6½ in. long, rubber band ¼ in. wide, string, stapler, scissors, pliers.

procedure

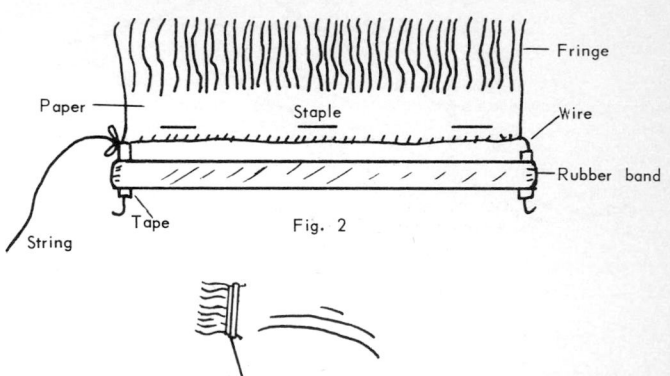

Fig. 2

1. Bend the wire up ½ in. at each end. Wrap the turned-up ends with adhesive paper or tape (Fig. 1).
2. Fold paper over wire and staple as illustrated. Fringe the edge of the folded paper (Fig. 2).
3. Wrap rubber band around each turned-up wire end. It should go across from wire to wire and be in tension (Fig. 2).
4. Tie string to wire at corner as in Fig. 3.
5. Holding the string in one hand, spin the bee through the air and hear it buzz (Fig. 3).

average time required

20 to 30 minutes. This project can be done by younger children if the wire foundation is prepared for them.

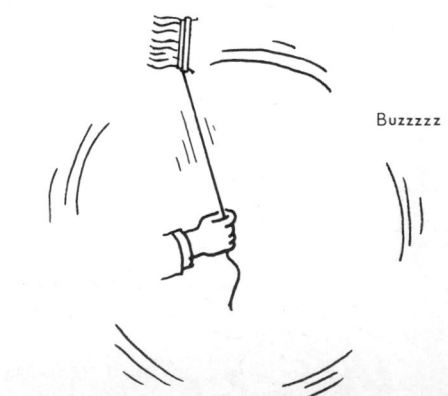

Fig. 3

colored-salt picture

Glue

Fig. 1

materials and tools

Salt, colored chalk, sheet of heavy colored paper.

procedure

1. On the foundation sheet trace with pencil the picture you wish to make (Fig. 1).
2. To color the salt, place the needed amount on a piece of paper and rub it with the colored chalk. Make up the colors before putting the picture together (Fig. 2).
3. Starting at the top of the picture, spread glue over a small area and spread the colored salt over the glue. For best results, do not try to glue and cover large areas at one time but stay within small areas. After the salt has settled, shake the paper to remove the excess salt.
4. Let dry before hanging.

average time required

40 minutes. Variations—instead of salt, use sawdust, sugar, crushed egg shell, or fine, clean sand.

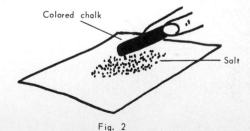

Colored chalk

Salt

Fig. 2

cord holder

materials and tools

A piece of heavy cloth, plastic material or oil cloth 12 by 6 in., yarn, paint, two large buttons, paper or cotton.

procedure

1. Draw the outline of a face (human or animal) upon the material. Cut out two matching faces.
2. Design and paint the face on one of the patterns. Make a hole at the nose from which the string can protrude.
3. With colored yarn stitch the two patterns together from point A by one ear, around the ear, down and around the chin and up and around the other ear to point B. Continue stitching from B to A, but sew only the front pattern. Do not connect the two pieces across the top. Be sure the patterned side of the material is outside on both pieces.
4. Stuff the ears with cotton or shredded paper.
5. Use four strands of yarn for the hanger. Attach it just above the ears.
6. Insert a ball of string through the opening at the top of the head and run the loose end through the hole in the nose.

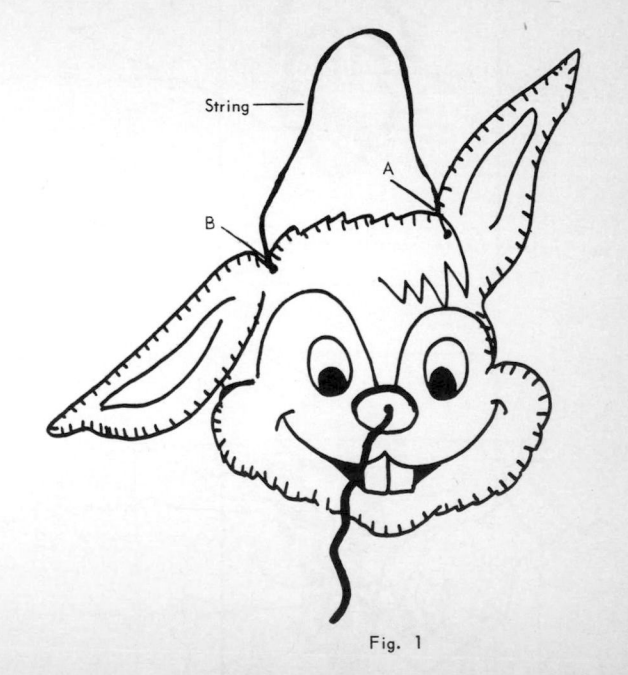

Fig. 1

crayon-eraser picture

materials and tools

Crayons, eraser, paper.

procedure

1. Color the edge of a sheet of paper with a heavy coating of colored crayon. The edge may be curved, straight, a design, or the outline of a picture (Fig. 1).
2. Place the crayon-colored paper in the desired position on the foundation paper.
3. Using an eraser, rub the crayon from the colored edge to the plain paper. This action will transfer the crayon color from the pattern to the plain paper (Figs. 1 and 2).
4. Any design or picture may be made by using a combination of colors and by moving the colored edge in different positions on the paper, then erasing.

average time required

40 minutes

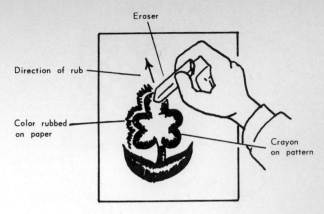

Eraser

Direction of rub

Color rubbed on paper

Crayon on pattern

Fig. 1

Fig. 2

crepe-paper basket

materials and tools

Cottage cheese carton, colored crepe paper, scissors, strip of cardboard 1 by 12 in., stapler, eggbeater.

procedure

1. Cut vertical strips in the carton about 1 in. apart, making sure there is an uneven number of strips. Cut the slits to within ¼ in. of the bottom of the carton (Fig. 1).
2. Cut strips of crepe paper 1½ in. wide. Twist the crepe paper by hand or fasten one end of a strip to an eggbeater, and, holding the other end securely, turn the beater until the paper is tightly twisted.
3. Beginning at the bottom of the slits, weave the crepe paper in and out. Continue around, making sure every row alternates. Push the strips tightly together. Cover the entire carton.
4. When adding a new strip of crepe paper, glue the ends together or fasten the ends on the inside by pushing them underneath the strip immediately below the new starting point.
5. Cover the outside base edge of the carton with a crepe paper strip. Glue this strip in place. Cover the top edge of the carton with a 2-in. strip of paper folded over the edge and glued in place (Fig. 2).

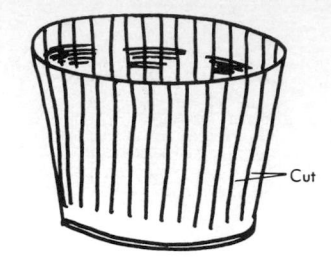

Fig. 1

Fig. 2

6. Wrap the cardboard strip with crepe paper to make the handle. Fasten the handle to the basket with a stapler (Fig. 2).
7. If a wider basket is desired, let the strips of the carton spread out as you weave.

average time required

90 minutes. The basket can also be made with untwisted crepe paper as in Fig. 2. Keep the untwisted crepe paper pushed down tightly as you weave. The basket can be decorated with artificial flowers fastened to the handle or side of the basket.

doll or puppet hat

materials and tools

A piece of felt (old felt hats can be washed and used for this purpose), glass tumbler, bottle or can with the proper diameter to make the hat fit the head of the doll, string, needle, thread, scissors, and a variety of materials suitable for decorating and trimming the hat.

procedure

1. Cut a circle of felt larger than the diameter of the can or bottle (Fig. 1).
2. Wet the piece of felt and stretch it tightly over the bottle or can to form the crown. Tie string around the felt to hold it at the desired depth of crown (Fig. 2).
3. If you want the brim to stand out, wrap a rolled piece of newspaper around the bottle beneath the brim, forcing it up into the desired position. Tie the roll of paper securely in place (Fig. 2). Let the hat dry overnight.
4. When felt is dry remove it from the bottle and trim it.

average time required

15 minutes to shape the felt. Time required to finish the hat will depend on the amount of trimming and decorating.

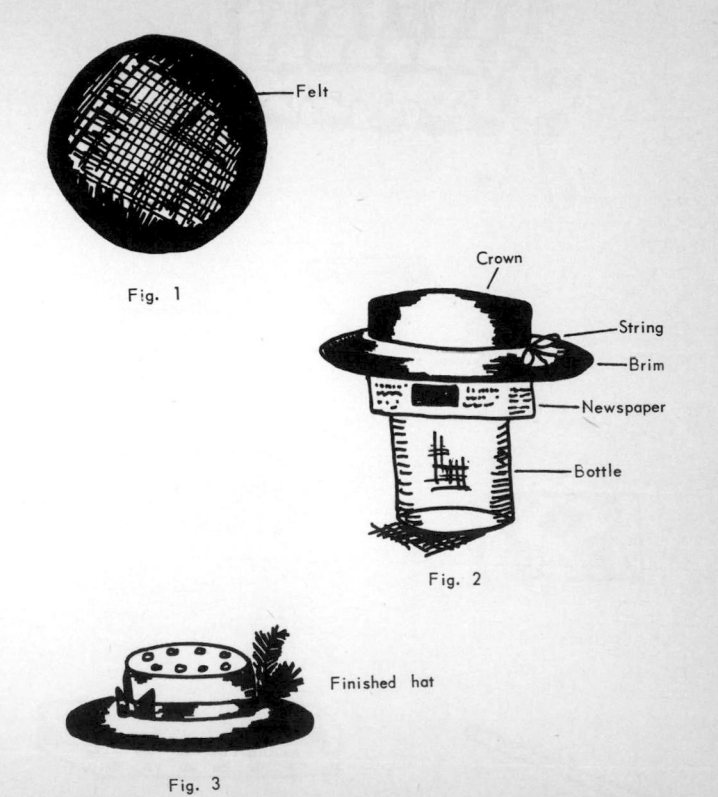

Felt

Fig. 1

Crown

String

Brim

Newspaper

Bottle

Fig. 2

Finished hat

Fig. 3

egg-carton caterpillar

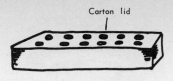

Fig. 1

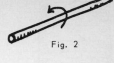

Fig. 2

materials and tools

One egg carton, crayons or poster paint, newspaper, piece of cardboard.

procedure

1. Cut leg holes in the outer edges of the carton lid about the size of a dime. Be sure these are placed to correspond with the twelve egg sections (Fig. 1).
2. Roll up a section of newspaper about 7 in. long and thick enough to fit into the leg holes. Bend this in the center and insert through two leg holes side by side. Bend at each end to resemble feet. Complete six of these until all leg holes have been filled, six on each side (Fig. 3).
3. Cut out a head from folded cardboard (Fig. 4). Glue it to front of the carton (Fig. 6).
4. Cut out a piece of cardboard to cover the back end of the caterpillar. Leave a flap on both sides of the rear section to allow for gluing it to the caterpillar's body (Figs. 5 and 6).
5. Paint or color caterpillar.

average time required

60 minutes

Fig. 3

Fig. 4

Fig. 5

Fig. 6

111

egg-cup tulips

materials and tools

A medium-size tin can half filled with sand, pipe cleaners, water colors or poster paint, green crepe paper or construction paper, one egg carton with molded cups in the bottom section.

procedure

1. Cut out several of the cups from the lower section of the egg carton (Fig. 1).
2. Paint the cups on the inside and the outside, then allow to dry (Fig. 4).
3. To make the center of the tulip, wrap yellow or black crepe paper around the end of a pipe cleaner (Fig. 3).
4. Make a small hole in the bottom of the tulip cup and put the pipe cleaner through the hole. Bend the stem slightly above and below the cup to hold it in place (Fig. 3).
5. Make two green leaves out of crepe paper or art paper about 3 in. long. Glue about half-way up from the bottom of the pipe cleaner stem (Fig. 4).
6. Wrap green paper over the entire pipe cleaner stem.
7. Arrange the flowers in the sand inside the tin can (Fig. 5).
8. Cover the outside of the tin can with crepe paper.

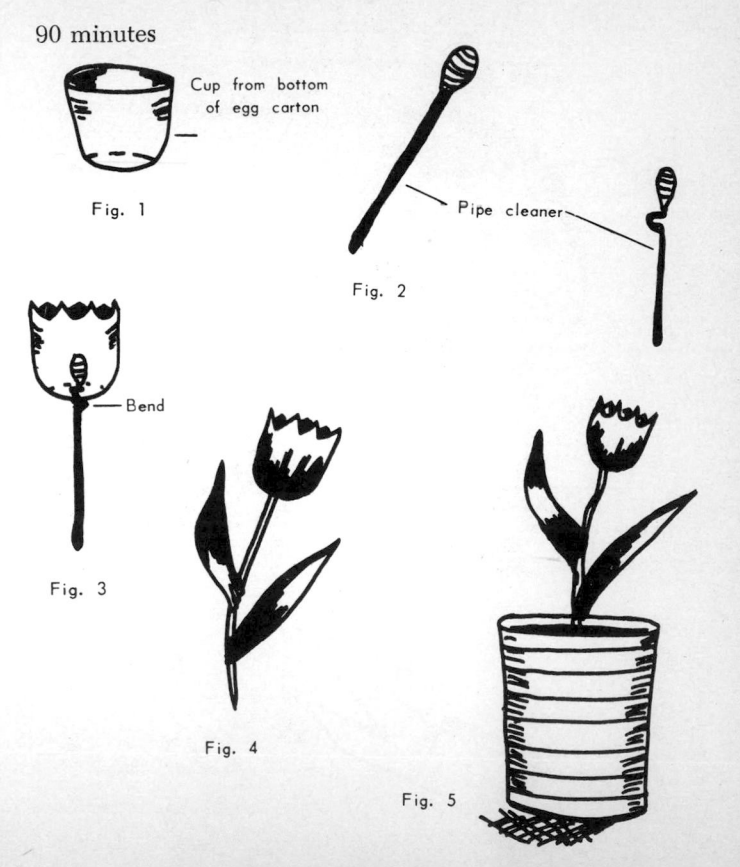

average time required

90 minutes

Cup from bottom of egg carton

Fig. 1

Pipe cleaner

Fig. 2

Bend

Fig. 3

Fig. 4

Fig. 5

glitter vase

materials and tools

Odd-shaped bottle, paint, glitter and sequins.

procedure

1. Paint a design on the bottle with a fast-drying enamel.
2. While the paint is still wet place the sequins on the design as desired, then sprinkle the rest of the design with glitter (Fig. 1).
3. After the paint is dry shake off the loose glitter.
4. If you wish, paint the rest of the bottle with a contrasting color (Fig. 2).

average time required

45 minutes

Fig. 1

Fig. 2

hobbyhorse

materials and tools

One old sock, yarn, string, old nylons, ink or felt dry ink marker, old broomstick, pieces of felt, heavy cord.

procedure

1. From the felt cut out two large round eyes and two smaller disks for the horse's nostrils. Sew them in place on the sock (Fig. 1).
2. Cut out the ears, fold the bottom edges under, and sew them in place (Fig. 1).
3. Ink-in the eyebrows and nose (Fig. 1).
4. Stuff the sock with old nylons or torn paper and place the neck of the sock on the broom handle and tie securely in place (Fig. 2).
5. Sew large, separate loops of yarn in place along the neck of the horse to make the mane. Clip each loop and tie securely (Fig. 2).
6. Run a heavy cord through the sides of the horse's mouth for reins and tie the ends as in Fig. 2.

average time required

60 minutes

114

Fold bottom edge

Sock

Fig. 1

Fig. 2

indian rattle

materials and tools

One round empty salt box, newspaper, five pebbles, wheat paste, poster paints, a round stick of wood about 12 in. long, string.

procedure

1. Tear newspapers into strips 1 to 2 in. wide.
2. Slide pebbles through opening into box (Fig. 2).
3. Place wooden handle along side of box and tie it securely in place with string (Fig. 2) or poke the handle through the center of the box and tie in place (Figs. 3 and 4). The first method guarantees a very secure handle—the other method looks more authentic.
4. Dip newspaper strips into paste and apply to the box until you have developed a ¼-in. layer of papier-mâché over the entire box (Fig. 5).

average time required

60 minutes of working time, not counting the drying time. You can use a can in place of the salt box. In this case apply only ⅛ in. of papier-mâché. After the rattle is completely dry, use crayons, poster paint, or enamels and decorate with Indian designs.

115

Fig. 1

Fig. 2

Fig. 3

Fig. 5

Fig. 4

kite

materials and tools

Ball of string, two sticks 24 and 30 in. long, paper, glue, waste cloth material.

procedure

1. Bind the 24-in. crossbar to the 30-in. stick at a point about 8 in. from the upper end, as shown in Fig. 1.
2. Fasten a piece of the string from point A to B to C to D to A (Fig. 2).
3. Lay the kite frame flat on a piece of paper and cut out a paper pattern ½ in. wider than the frame.
4. Fold the ½-in. paper edge over the string and glue it down.
5. Turn the kite over so that the wooden braces are on the bottom and the paper side is facing you and tie a piece of string tightly from D to B. Pull the string tight enough to curve the crossbrace stick so that it bows out about 4 in. from the string (Fig. 3).
6. Punch holes through the paper at points 1 and 2. The number 1 hole is approximately 3 in. from point A and the number 2 hole is placed about 7 in. above point C (Fig. 4). Tie a guide string to the long stick at point 1 and bring it through the hole and down the front of the kite, through the hole at point 2, and tie it to the brace at this point. Leave this string loose.

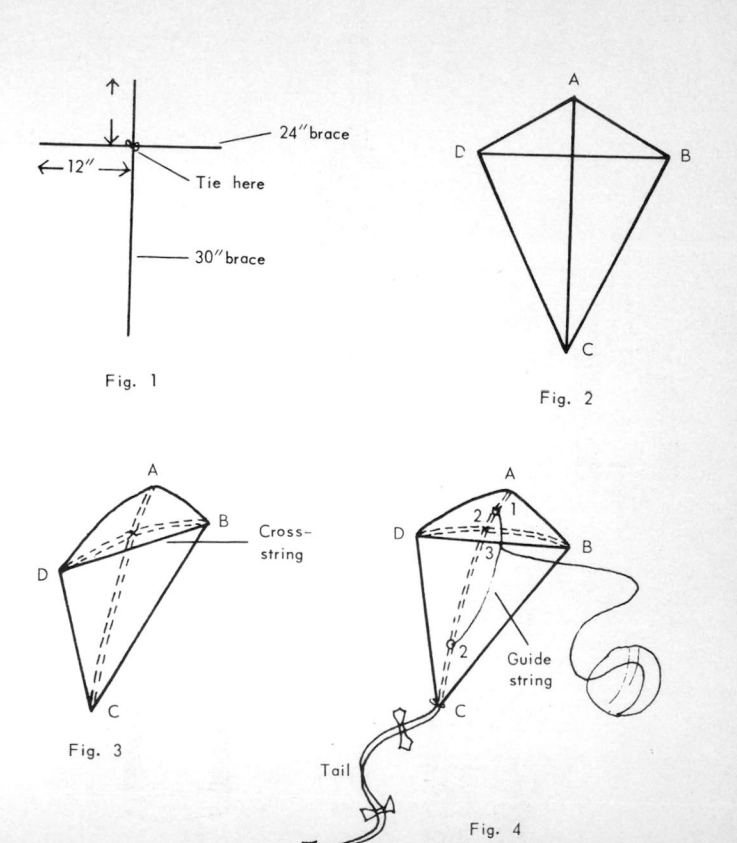

Fig. 1

Fig. 2

Fig. 3

Fig. 4

116

7. Attach the ball of string to the guide string at point 3 (Fig. 4).
8. Add a tail of cloth about ½ in. wide and from 5 to 7 ft. long (Fig. 4). Make the tail longer if the kite tips and dips too much. To do this, simply tie on additional lengths of cloth.

average time required

60 minutes

moving-shadow figures

materials and tools

Cardboard, dark-colored construction paper, sheet of thin white paper, glue or staples.

procedure

1. Cut out a cardboard picture frame, 9 by 8 in. (Fig. 1).
2. Glue or staple white piece of paper to the back of the frame (Fig. 2).
3. Decide upon the theme of the picture, draw the figure of an animal, bird, or person on the dark-colored paper, and cut it out. Do not make the figure overly fat or too big (Fig. 3).
4. Cut out two tabs of construction paper about 1 in. long and ¼ in. wide. Bend or fold them three times like an accordion (Fig. 4).
5. Glue or staple the accordion tabs to the rear of the cutout figure—one at the top and one at the bottom (Fig. 5).
6. Glue the pads to the back of the picture (Fig. 5).
7. To operate, turn out the lights and hold the picture in front of you with the figure facing you. Move a lighted flashlight back and forth and around between you and the picture, and the figure, when seen from the other side, will move, fly, or dance (Fig. 6).

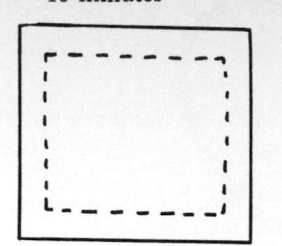

Fig. 1

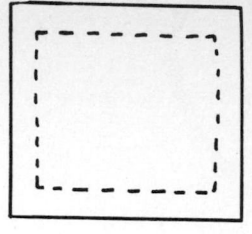

Fig. 2

Fig. 3

Fig. 4

Front of picture

Fig. 5

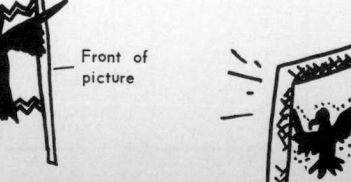
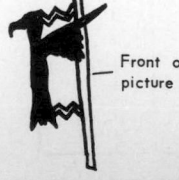

paper beads

materials and tools

Paper (construction paper, wallpaper, or magazine pages), toothpicks, glue, string, shellac (if desired).

procedure

1. Cut paper in strips. Width and length of the paper determines the size of the bead (Fig. 1).
2. Tapered strips of paper will produce a barrel-shaped bead; strips cut straight will produce a cylindrical bead (Figs. 5 and 6).
3. Cover one side of the paper strip with glue and place the toothpick at one end. Roll tightly into a compact unit (Figs. 2, 3, and 4).
4. Remove the toothpick before the bead dries. Let the bead dry thoroughly. Paint or shellac the beads after they have dried. Shellac darkens the color of the beads.
5. String beads according to designs and colors (Fig. 7).

average time required

40 to 60 minutes, depending upon the length of the strand. Beads can be rolled on a nail. If this is done, make the strips of paper longer than those required above. Beads made this way can be threaded on yarn, with or without a knot between them.

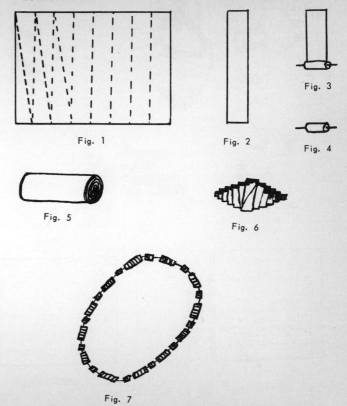

Fig. 1

Fig. 2

Fig. 3

Fig. 4

Fig. 5

Fig. 6

Fig. 7

parachute

30 minutes

materials and tools

An 8-in. square of lightweight cloth, a small weight such as a nail or washer, eight pieces of string about 9 in. long.

procedure

1. Number with a pencil the four corners of the cloth (**Fig. 1**). Fold the cloth three times by bringing corner 1 over to 3, corner 2 to 4, then fold the double corners together by bringing 1 and 3 down to the 2 and 4 corners (Figs. 1, 2, 3, and 4).
2. Measure the distance from A to B and along side AC mark off this same distance and designate this point as D. Draw a rounding line from point D to B and cut along this line to round off the edges of the parachute.
3. Punch a hole half way between the points D and B and ½ in. from the rounded edge of the cloth (Fig. 4).
4. Unfold the cloth and tie the strings in each of the holes. Tie the other ends of the strings to the weight (Figs. 5 and 6).
5. To operate the parachute—without twisting the strings—place the weight at point W (Fig. 6). Fold the parachute neatly around the weight and then throw it into the air. If it is folded correctly it will open, fill with air, and slowly float to the ground.

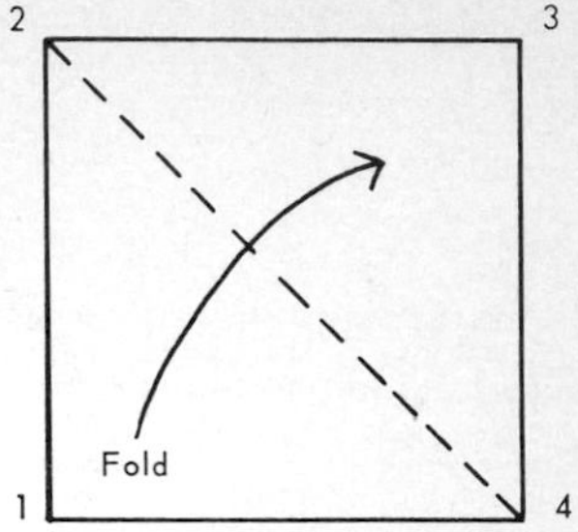

Fig. 1

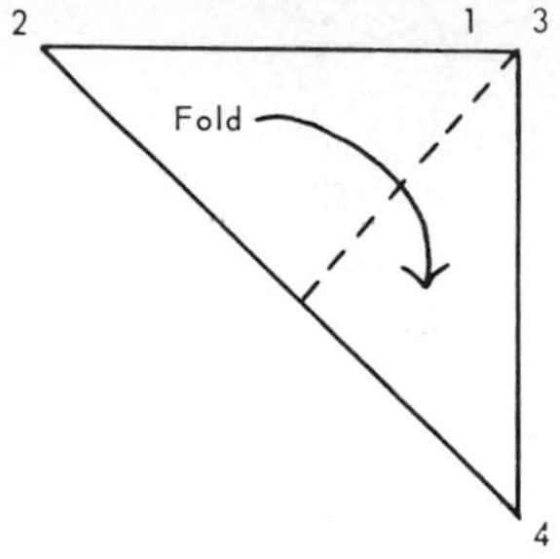

Fig. 2

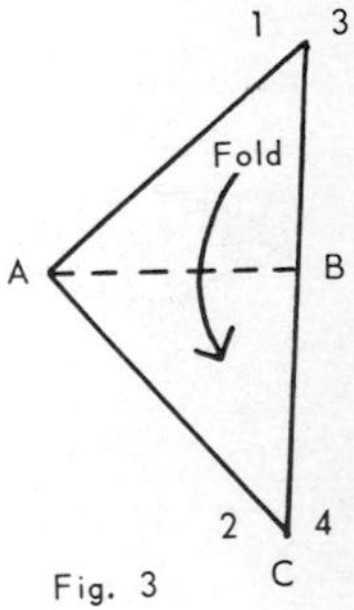

Fig. 3

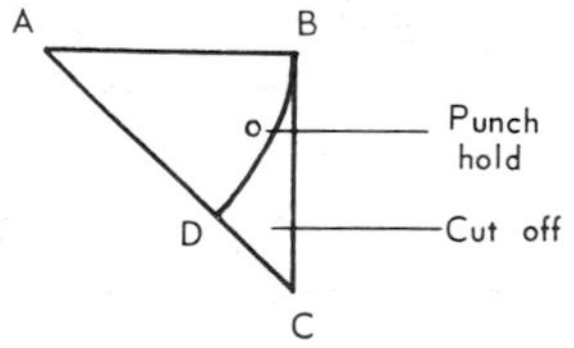

Fig. 4

Punch hold

Cut off

Material

Strings

Weight

Fig. 5

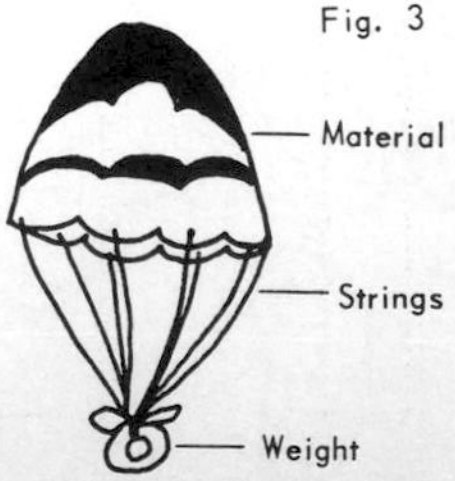

Fig. 6

peanut man

materials and tools

Five large peanuts; one small, single-section peanut; enamel or felt dry ink marker; fine sharp needle; thread.

procedure

1. Sew the single peanut (head) to one of the larger double nuts (body) with thread (Fig. 1).
2. Sew arms to the body (Fig. 2).
3. Sew legs to the body (Fig. 3).
4. Paint face and the rest of the body as desired.

average time required

20 minutes

Fig. 1

Fig. 2

Fig. 3

plaster picture frame

materials and tools

Small aluminum-foil individual pie tin, plaster of paris, a small picture, a paper clip, bowl, water, lacquer.

procedure

1. Mix plaster and water to a thick consistency.
2. Place the picture face down in the bottom of the pie tin (Fig. 1).
3. Spread the plaster over the picture until it is about ½ in. thick (Fig. 2).
4. Shape the paper clip as in Fig. 3 and insert it into the soft plaster (Fig. 2).
5. Allow the plaster to dry overnight. To remove the plaster from the tinfoil, hold it upside down in your hand and lightly tap it around the edges. After the plaster has been removed, sand down the edges or smooth them with a knife blade.
6. Lacquer and frame the picture and when dry hang it on the wall.

average time required

30 minutes

Place picture here face down

Fig. 1

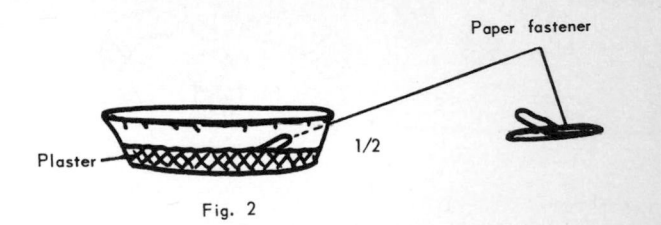

Paper fastener

Plaster

1/2

Fig. 2

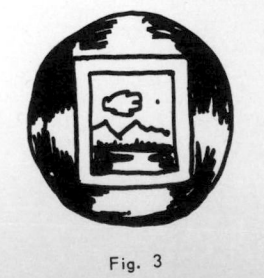

Fig. 3

powered houseboat

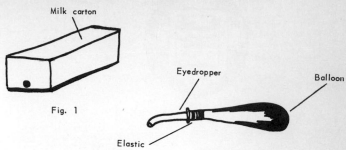

Milk carton

Fig. 1

Eyedropper

Balloon

Elastic

Fig. 2

materials and tools

A one-quart milk carton, one long rubber balloon, one glass section from an eyedropper, glue, elastic band.

procedure

1. Be sure the milk carton is clean, then cut a small hole close to one side on the bottom of the carton (Fig. 1).
2. Insert the large end of the eye dropper into the balloon and wrap tightly with elastic band so that it is airtight (Fig. 2).
3. Holding the balloon on the opposite end from the eyedropper, dangle the dropper down through the top of the carton and into the hole at the bottom. Close the top of the carton and fasten with tape or staples.
4. Pull the dropper tube about 1 in. through the hole. Point it downward at a 30° angle (Fig. 3). Turn the carton on its side and scrape the top side free of wax; then glue paper chimneys to it for smoke stacks (Fig. 4).
5. Blow up the balloon through the eyedropper, place your finger over the hole in the dropper until the carton is placed in water. When your finger is removed from the hole, the escaping air will propel the boat through the water (Fig. 4).

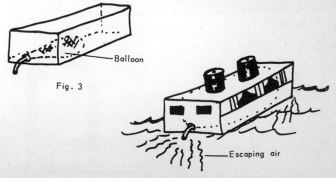

Balloon

Fig. 3

Escaping air

Fig. 4

123

propelled boat

materials and tools

A light piece of wood 3 by 6 by ¼ in., a saw, two elastic bands, a wooden tongue depressor, knife.

procedure

1. Cut the boat pattern out of the piece of wood (Fig. 1).
2. Cut the propeller out of the tongue depressor with a knife (Fig. 2).
3. Cut notches in the end of the boat where the elastic bands will be placed. Stretch the elastic bands and place them around the notched areas, then place the propeller between them. Sometimes it is necessary to tie the elastic bands on each side of the propeller with a piece of string so it will not slip out (Fig. 3).
4. To operate the boat simply wind up the propeller, place the boat in the water, and release it. Wind the propeller by turning it away from the boat (Fig. 3).

average time required

90 minutes

124

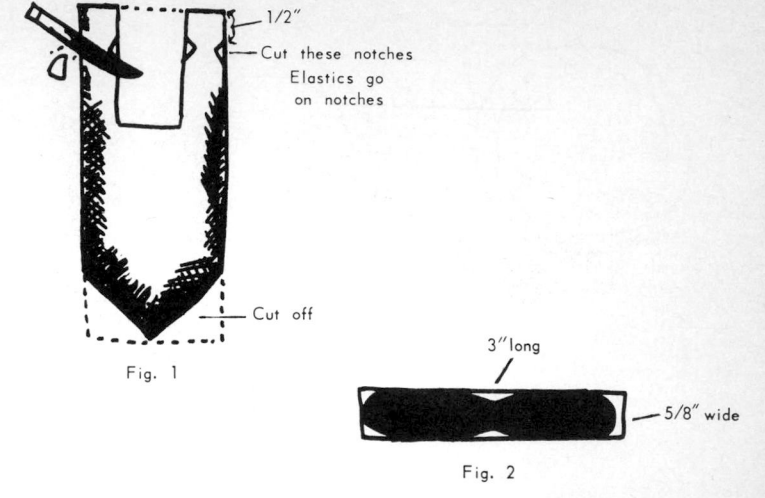

1/2"
Cut these notches
Elastics go on notches
Cut off

Fig. 1

3" long
5/8" wide

Fig. 2

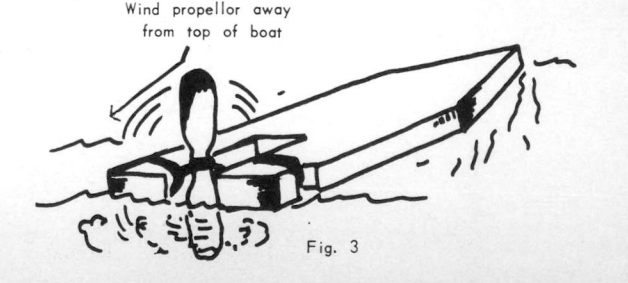

Wind propellor away from top of boat

Fig. 3

ring toss

materials and tools

A section of an old broom or mop handle or a round piece of wood 10 in. long with a 1 in. diameter, string, paint if desired, a round ring or stiff rope from which to make a ring.

procedure

1. Cut off a 10-in. section of the broom handle and point one end (Fig. 1).
2. Cut two notches on either side of the stick as in the diagram (Fig. 1).
3. Tie a 12-in. piece of string around the rod at the point of the notches. The notches will prevent the string from slipping forward on the rod.
4. Tie the ring to the end of the string.
5. To operate, hold the rod at the thick end, letting the ring hang down. Using arm, hand, and wrist actions, swing the ring forward and up and attempt to catch the ring on the pointed end of the rod.
6. To make a rope ring use a 10-in. section of stiff ¼- to ½-in. rope. Taper the ends of the rope and bring them together and overlap them about ½ in. Using string or adhesive tape, bind the ends securely together (Figs. 2 and 3).

125

25 minutes

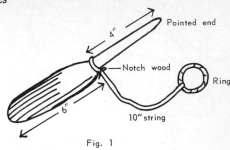

Fig. 1

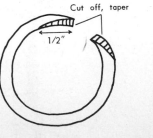

Fig. 2

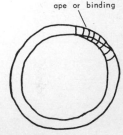

Fig. 3

spatter painting

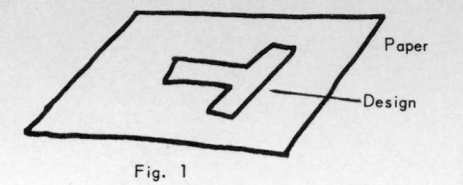

Fig. 1

materials and tools

Ink, toothbrush, piece of screen 4 by 4 in., paper, design.

procedure

1. Draw and cut out a design and place it in the desired position on the foundation paper (Fig. 1). To hold it in place while you are using the spatter, use two or three small loops of Scotch tape directly underneath the design and press securely onto the foundation.
2. Dip brush in ink. To prevent heavy drops from falling on the paper, use small amounts of ink at a time.
3. Hold the screen about 2 in. above the paper (Fig. 2).
4. Brush the screen with the inked brush until the desired color is obtained.
5. Let the ink dry, then remove the design and the image will be left on the paper (Fig. 3).

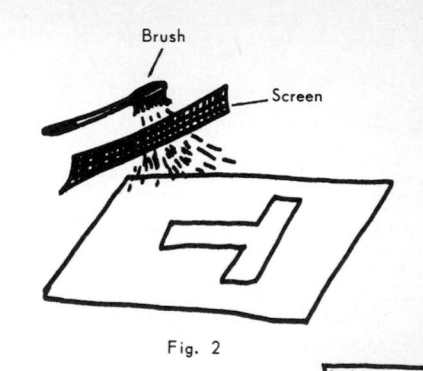

Fig. 2

average time required

30 minutes

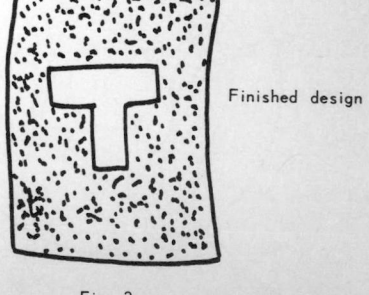

Fig. 3

spool knitting

materials and tools

One large spool about 2 in. long with a large center hole, four small-headed nails about ½ in. long, a ball of wool, cord or string, a nail or crochet hook, hammer.

procedure

1. Drive the nails into the top of the spool as in Fig. 1. They should stand about ⅝6 in. above the wood.
2. Drop the end of the cord through the hole as in Fig. 1. Be sure to leave about 4 in. of the cord showing from the bottom hole.
3. Wrap the string from one nail to the next in the following manner: wrap the cord counterclockwise around the first nail so that the cord is over itself as you proceed to encircle nail #2. Continue this circling until you have looped each nail once (Fig. 2).
4. Continue the cord around the outside of the nails and on top of the first loops. Do not loop the cord completely around the nails the second time around (Fig. 2).
5. Push the knitting nail into the lower loop as in Fig. 2 (position, nail #1) and pull the lower loop of the cord out and up and over the second, or top, cord, and then up and over

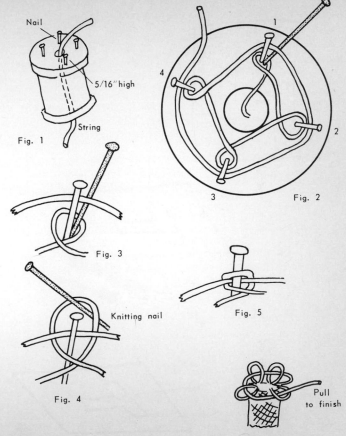

Fig. 1

Nail

5/16" high

String

Fig. 2

1

4

2

3

Fig. 3

Fig. 4

Knitting nail

Fig. 5

Fig. 6

Pull to finish

the head of nail #1. Allow the loop to fall to the center of the spool (Figs. 3, 4, and 5).

6. Continue clockwise around the top of the spool, pulling the lower loop out, up, and over each nail until you have completed looping the four nails. Hold the spool in your left hand and with the right grasp the short tail of cord hanging below the spool and give it a light tug. As you continue weaving over the four nails and tugging the tail cord, be sure to keep the pressure of the pull the same every time. This will insure an even braid with equal stitches.

7. Continue wrapping the cord around the four nails and the action of pulling the under cord out and over the top cord and over the nail head. Do not forget the even tug on the tail. In a short time the braid will appear from the bottom of the spool. Continue weaving until braid is the desired length.

8. To finish braid, slip the last four loops off the nails. Cut the cord between the ball of cord and the loops. Leave enough cord so that you can slip it through each string loop, one after another, going counterclockwise. When completed, pull the loose end and tighten the loops to finish the braid (Fig. 4).

average time required

Varies according to the length of the braid.

stocking hand puppets

materials and tools

Old sock, colored yarn, colored cloth.

procedure

1. Turn the sock inside out and cut a mouth in the sock. This is a slit around the toe of the sock (Fig. 1).
2. Select a solid color from the colored cloth and cut out a lining for the puppet's mouth (Fig. 2).
3. Sew the mouth lining in place·and turn the sock right side out (Fig. 3).
4. Using different colored materials, cut out ears, tongue, eyes, eyebrows, and nostrils, and sew them in place (Fig. 3). Allow children to use their own imagination to develop many different faces (snake, giraffe, dog, alligator, cat, bird, human, etc.).
5. Use yarn to make hair or fringe.
6. To operate, place the hand in the sock with the thumb in the lower-jaw and fingers in the upper-jaw section. Move fingers and open and close your hand to get the required action.

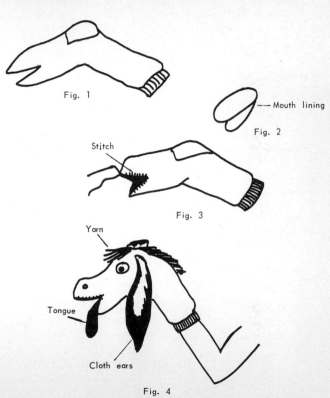

Fig. 1

Mouth lining

Fig. 2

Stitch

Fig. 3

Yarn

Tongue

Cloth ears

Fig. 4

stuffed rubber doll

materials and tools

A discarded rubber tire tube, yarn, scissors, needles (large enough to thread yarn), crayons, ink or felt dry ink marker, newspaper, cotton, old nylons, cloth scraps or torn newspaper.

procedure

1. Make a pattern such as a gingerbread boy on a piece of newspaper (Fig. 1).
2. Cut out two pieces of rubber tubing large enough to fit your pattern. Mark the pattern on one of the pieces of tubing with ink or crayon, place the two sides of the tubing together with the shiny side showing on each, then cut the pattern on both pieces at once to be sure that both pieces are identical (Fig. 2).
3. Keep the pieces together as they were when you cut them out. Begin sewing them together with yarn and keep stitching until only part of the right arm and the whole head remain to be stitched (Fig. 3).
4. Stuff the doll with cotton, cloth scraps, or newspaper and complete the stitching. When the doll is completely stitched draw the features for the face, or stitch them with yarn. Decorate as desired (Fig. 4).

average time required

90 minutes. This procedure may be used to make any type of doll, figure, or animal. Felt or buttons can be used for eyes and other trim, and yarn can be used for hair.

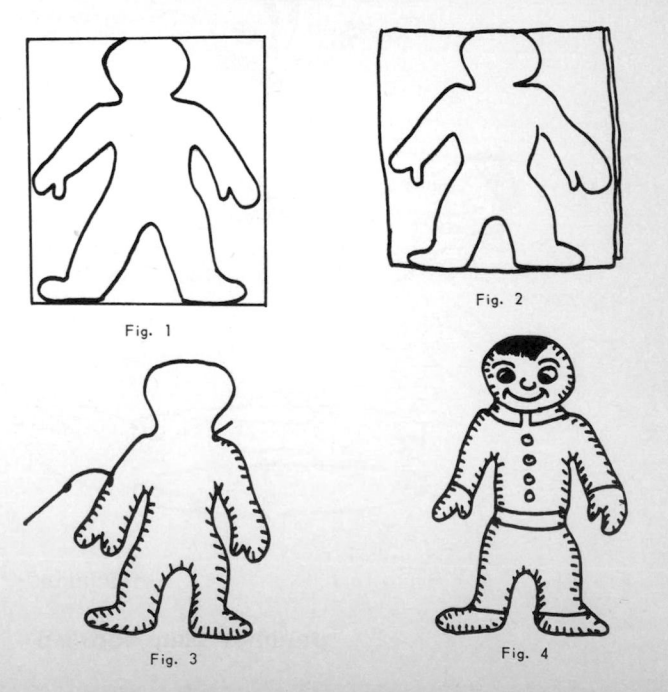

Fig. 1

Fig. 2

Fig. 3

Fig. 4

tambourine

materials and tools

A round cereal box lid, four round-headed paper fasteners, hammer, twelve pop bottle caps, crayons, large nail, crepe paper streamers or ribbons.

procedure

1. Cut four ½-in. squares at even intervals around the side of the lid (Fig. 1).
2. Punch four holes on top of the lid ¼ in. from the edge to correspond with the side openings (Fig. 1).
3. Remove the cork and flatten the soda pop bottle caps with a hammer (Fig. 2).
4. Punch a hole in the center of each cap with a large nail (Fig. 2).
5. Put a paper fastener through three caps and put the end of it up through one of the holes in the top of the lid. Spread the fastener's legs to hold it in place. Fasten it loosely so that the caps are free to jingle. Follow this procedure for each of the holes in the lid. Part of the bottle caps should stick out of the side openings (Figs. 3 and 4).
6. Decorate with crayons and attach streamers (Fig. 4).

average time required

45 minutes

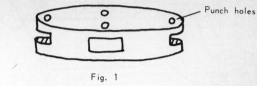

Fig. 1

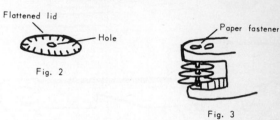

Fig. 2

Fig. 3

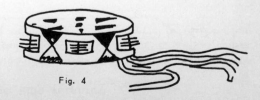

Fig. 4

willow whistle

materials and tools

A sharp pocket knife and a 5-in. section of a straight branch from a green willow tree. The section must be free from knot-holes and buds, and it should be approximately ¾ in. in diameter.

procedure

1. Using your knife, cut a ring in the bark of the limb at A. Cut the bark only and do not cut the woody part of the branch (Fig. 1).
2. Cut out a notch at C about ⅜ in. long and about ¼ in. deep. This should be approximately ½ in. from the mouth end.
3. With the knife handle, tap firmly all of the bark that is going to be stripped off. This is between points A and D. Tap the bark for a short time and then dip it into lukewarm water. This helps to loosen the bark from the wood. Repeat this action several times before attempting to turn or twist the bark from the wood. Remove the bark when it becomes loose (Fig. 3). Be sure not to tap or twist the bark so hard that you damage or break it.
4. After removing the bark, increase the size of the cut in the wood at C to approximately ⅜ in. deep and about ¾ in. long (Fig. 2). This opening should be about one-half the depth of the diameter of the piece of wood.
5. Cut off section B (Fig. 1). Replace the bark and carefully

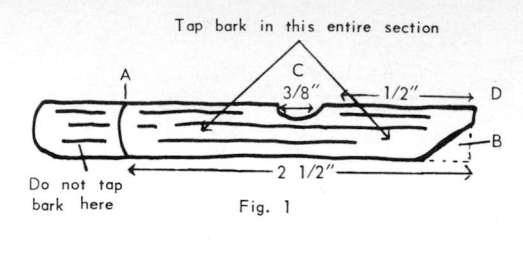

Tap bark in this entire section

C
3/8"   1/2"

A   D
B

Do not tap bark here

2 1/2"

Fig. 1

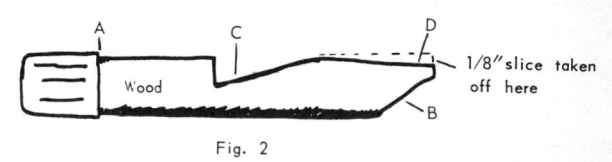

A   C   D
Wood   1/8" slice taken off here
B

Fig. 2

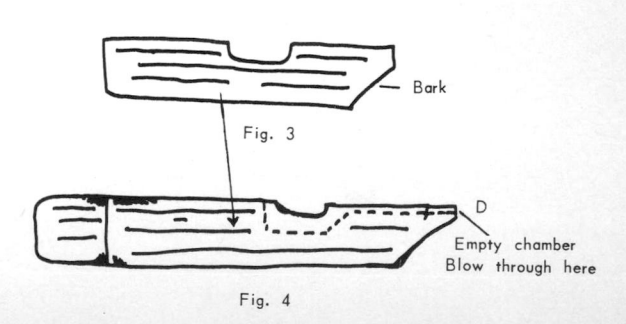

Bark

Fig. 3

D
Empty chamber
Blow through here

Fig. 4

132

trim the bark to fit the wooden mouthpiece.

6. Remove the bark again and cut the mouthpiece down about ⅛ in. (Fig. 2). Do not make any more cuts in the bark.

7. Replace the bark, place the tapered end into the mouth, and blow air through D to make the whistling sound (Fig. 4).

average time required

45 minutes

part four   fourth-grade ages

fourth-grade ages

Acrobat **137**

Beanie Cap **139**

Bug Cage **140**

Case for Glasses,
Pens, or Pencils **141**

Confetti or Torn-
paper Pictures **142**

Decorated Puzzle
Sticks **143**

Dyed-rice Mosaic **146**

Earth Weather
Satellite **148**

Fish Kite **150**

Handy Miniature
Scorekeeper **152**

Hot Pad **153**

Jitterbugs **155**

Lighthouse **156**

Log Cabin **157**

Paper-napkin
Holder **159**

Papier-mâché
Puppets or Dolls **160**

Pencil Holder **162**

Rope Belt **163**

Rubber-headed
Drum **165**

Rustic Picture
Frame **167**

Snapshot Holder **168**

Spoon Animals **170**

Spool Penholder **171**

Sword Pins **172**

Table Croquet **174**

Wheel Runner **175**

Wrapped Wire or
Rod Figures **176**

acrobat

materials and tools

A sheet of lightweight cardboard, a sheet of white paper, strong cord, crayons or colored felt dry ink markers, scissors, paper punch.

procedure

1. Draw the figure and limbs of the acrobat on the sheet of paper (Fig. 1). Remember to make the sections of the legs and arms extra long because of the needed overlap for fastening together. The figure can be any size, but be sure to have the other parts proportional.
2. Cut out the body sections and trace them on cardboard. Cut out the cardboard sections.
3. On each body section, mark the required string holes and punch them out with a nail, large needle, or paper punch (Fig. 1).
4. Tie the leg and arm sections together by threading a short piece of string through the matching holes and making a large knot on each side. Using the same method, tie the legs and arms to the body section (Figs. 2 and 3).
5. At the rear of the figure, attach the arms to each other by running a short loose string from hole C in one arm to hole C in the other arm. This string should be loose enough to allow the arms to hang normally. In the same manner attach

137

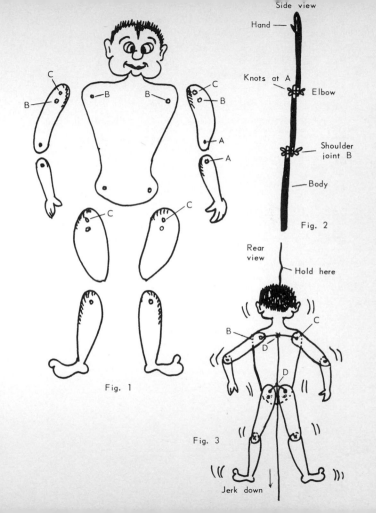

Fig. 1

Fig. 2

Fig. 3

a string from C to C on the leg sections (Figs. 1 and 3).

6. At the top of the head attach a short holding string (Fig. 3).
7. Fasten an 18-in. piece of string to the center of each of the arm and leg cross strings at points D and D as in Fig. 3. Be sure to leave several inches of the string hanging below the body to be used for activating the figure.
8. To operate, hold the head string in one hand and jerk on the action string. This will cause the arms and legs to dance erratically.

average time required

60 minutes

beanie cap

materials and tools

Felt, yarn, colored buttons, bottle caps, paper punch, scissors.

procedure

1. Using the pattern in Fig. 1, cut out six pieces of felt. These dimensions fit an average-size head. Adjust slightly for smaller or larger children.
2. Using the same pattern, mark where the holes are to be punched on each section of felt, then punch out the holes with a paper punch. Be sure the holes are placed the same on each section.
3. With a 20-in. piece of yarn, interlace the sections of the beanie together, starting from the bottom. Bring the pieces of yarn up through each hole. Leave the ends loose at the top (Figs. 2 and 3).
4. When all the sections are laced together, wind a small piece of yarn around the loose ends at the top and tie securely. Trim the ends evenly to about 1-in. lengths.
5. If desired, sew on brightly colored buttons, or remove the cork from the bottle caps and attach the caps by putting the corks on the opposite side of the cloth and pressing together.

139

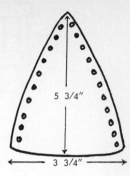

5 3/4"

3 3/4"

Fig. 1

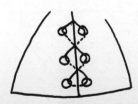

Fig. 2

Fig. 3

bug cage

materials and tools

A medium-size piece of foam plastic, straight pins, razor blade, colored bead, fine sandpaper.

procedure

1. From foam plastic cut out a block about ⅜ in. thick and 2½ by 2½ in. square. This is the bottom of the cage (Fig. 1).
2. From plastic foam make the top section. Make it domed, steepled, or any shape you wish (Fig. 2).
3. Place the bead on a pin and push the pin into the top of the cage. If you wish, make a small paper flag, place it on the pin, and insert on top of the cage (Fig. 3).
4. Stick pins down through the top section and into the bottom section for cage bars. Be sure that the pins are close enough together to hold your bug. If you wish legs on the cage, place four pins on the bottom of the four corners of the plastic material.
5. To place the bug in the cage, pull two bar pins partially out of their holes to form a door. Replace the pins after the bug has been enclosed.
6. Place food in the cage for insects. A dead fly for a spider, for example, or grass for a grasshopper.

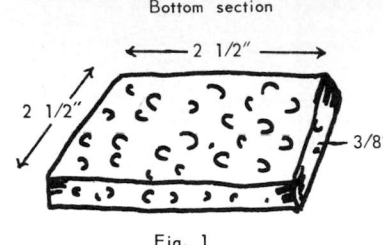

Bottom section

← 2 1/2″ →

2 1/2″

3/8″

Fig. 1

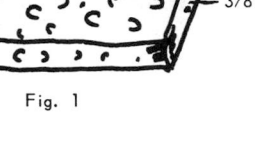

Top section

Fig. 2

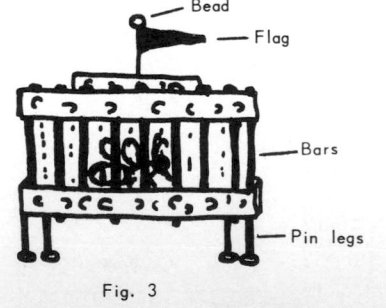

Bead

Flag

Bars

Pin legs

Fig. 3

case for glasses, pens, or pencils

materials and tools

Cardboard, plastic material, leatherette or felt, scissors, glue, needle or bobby pin, yarn or plastic lacing.

procedure

1. Cut out two pieces of plastic or felt material 6½ by 3 in. (Fig. 1).
2. Cut out two pieces of cardboard slightly smaller than the material. This is for lining the case (Fig. 2).
3. Glue the cardboard and material together (Fig. 3).
4. Punch holes around the sides and one end of both pieces of the case (Fig. 4).
5. Sew through the holes in the material with the yarn or lacing (Fig. 5).

average time required

60 minutes. You can make a case for letters or valuable papers by cutting the material 7 by 3¾ in. Scrap plastic materials can be obtained from automobile upholstering shops.

141

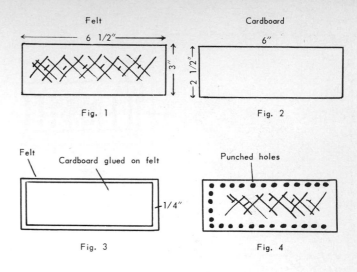

Fig. 1

Fig. 2

Fig. 3

Fig. 4

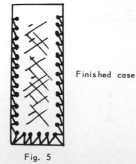

Finished case

Fig. 5

confetti or torn-paper pictures

materials and tools

Colored paper (several colors), paper punch, toothpicks, paste or glue, scissors, mounting paper (preferably a color darker than the confetti).

procedure

1. On the mounting paper outline the desired picture or design (Fig. 1).
2. Punch or tear out the confetti from the colored sheets of paper.
3. Apply paste to the tiny shapes and with a toothpick press them into place. If you are covering a large area, smear it with glue and press the confetti to the sticky surface and arrange the pieces in place (Fig. 2).
4. To preserve the picture, cover it with shellac; this will prevent the confetti from loosening and falling off.

average time required

40 to 60 minutes, depending on the size of the picture.

Fig. 1

Fig. 2

decorated puzzle sticks

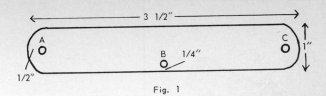

Fig. 1

materials and tools

A piece of thin plywood 3½ by 1 in., a piece of plywood 4 by 1¼ in., cord, three buttons or small washers, sandpaper, a knife with a narrow blade, felt stick dry ink markers.

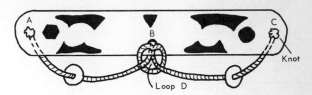

Fig. 2

procedure

1. Follow the illustrations and construct the two puzzle sticks. Sand sticks until they are smooth and decorate them as desired (Figs. 1 and 4).

2. To thread the puzzle stick (Fig. 1), tie a heavy knot at the end of a 13-in. string. Thread the string through the left hole in the stick and place a washer on the string. Bring the string across the back of the stick and thread it through center hole B. Thread the end of the string behind the string section that crosses from A to B and again take it through hole B, forming loop D. Bring the string down the back of the stick and up through loop D; now place another washer on the cord. Thread the cord through hole C from the rear to the front and tie a heavy knot in the end of the cord.

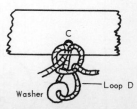

Fig. 3

3. The trick of the puzzle is to work the washers so they are both on the same side of hole B.

Solution: Slide the right washer to the left along the string and push it through loop D (Fig. 3). Grasp the string from behind the stick and pull on it until loop D slides through the hole B. This places loop D to the rear of the stick with the washer at the bottom of the D loop. The washer is now in position to slide to the left along the string to the left side of loop D. Move it over and pull loop D back to its original position. The washer is still in loop D but on the string running from A to B. Slide the washer around and through the loop to the left; you now have the two washers together on the left side of the stick. To separate the two washers, reverse the procedure.

4. To make the second puzzle stick, bore two holes 1 in. from each end of the stick and thread the cord through the holes as shown in Fig. 4. To solve the puzzle remove the string from the stick without breaking or untying it. Notice that the knot in the string is at the middle of the stick and the length of the string from the knot to the button is 4 in.

Solution: Pull all the slack string up through the bottom hole until you can push the knot through the top hole. Slide the right side of the loop that encircles the stick over to the left side. This changes the position of the loop. It is now on the left side of the stick rather than over the top (Fig. 5). Slide this new loop down the string toward the knot. Take it down past the knot and pass it through the bottom hole. Do not twist the loop while doing this. Slip the button or washer through the loop. Pull on the button and the entire string will slide from the stick. If you do not have enough

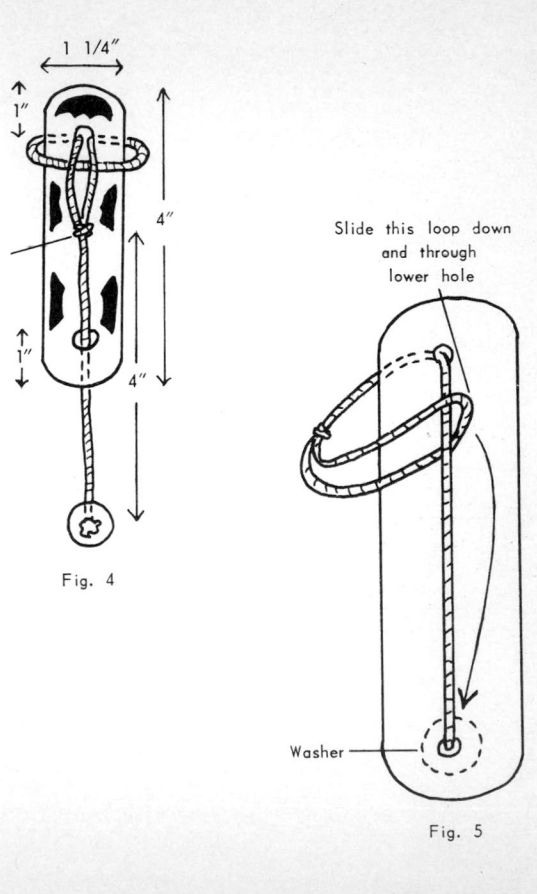

Fig. 4

Slide this loop down
and through
lower hole

Washer

Fig. 5

loop protruding through the hole to allow the button to slip through it, you will need to rethread the stick with a longer string. This problem sometimes occurs if the button or washer placed at the end of the string is large. Reverse the process to return the string and button to their original positions.

average time required

40 minutes to make both projects and decorate if the sticks are cut to size beforehand.

dyed-rice mosaic

materials and tools

Long-grain rice (regular rice is preferable to five-minute rice, which breaks very easily), food coloring or Easter egg dye, ¼-in.-thick plywood (or heavy cardboard) of any size, glue, dark-dyed butcher's twine or heavy cord, clear shellac, varnish and brush.

procedure

1. Draw a picture on paper that is the same size as the plywood. Transfer the picture onto the wood. With dark cord and glue, outline the picture. Apply the glue over a small section at a time and press the cord until the glue sets (Fig. 1).
2. Fill the entire picture with rice colored to your choice. Spread glue over a small area at a time and work only with one color at a time (Fig. 2).
3. After the picture is completed and thoroughly dried, apply shellac or varnish over all and allow to dry again (Fig. 3). The varnish or shellac gives a gloss to the picture and holds the rice.

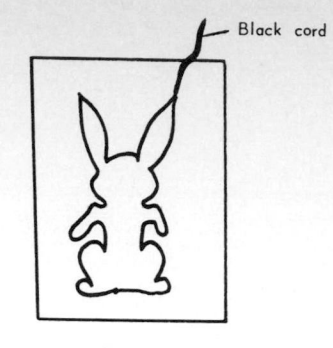

Black cord

Fig. 1

Fig. 2

Fig. 3

146

average time required

40 minutes for a small picture if the rice is precolored. To color the rice put it in a glass container with a lid, add a few drops of coloring, and shake vigorously. Spread it in a thin layer on newspaper and let it dry thoroughly. Store in a dry, covered, glass jar.

earth weather satellite

materials and tools

A small block of foam plastic, a ball of cotton, fast-drying glue, six wooden matches or round toothpicks, about 6 in. of plastic or rubber tubing approximately ⅜ in. in diameter, a razor blade or pocket knife, sandpaper.

procedure

1. Carve a ball out of the foam plastic about the size of a ping-pong ball. Smooth it with sandpaper.
2. Using the matches or round toothpicks, make six sticks ¾ in. long and ⅛ in. thick (Fig. 1).
3. Push the sticks at even intervals into the foam plastic ball (Fig. 2).
4. To operate the satellite, place it on the end of the tube with one of the sticks inserted in the hole of the tube. Place the other end of the tube in your mouth and blow a steady stream of air through it. (Do not blow too hard.) As the satellite slowly rises, increase the air pressure. After the ball is in the air, adjust the air stream to keep the ball afloat (Fig. 3).

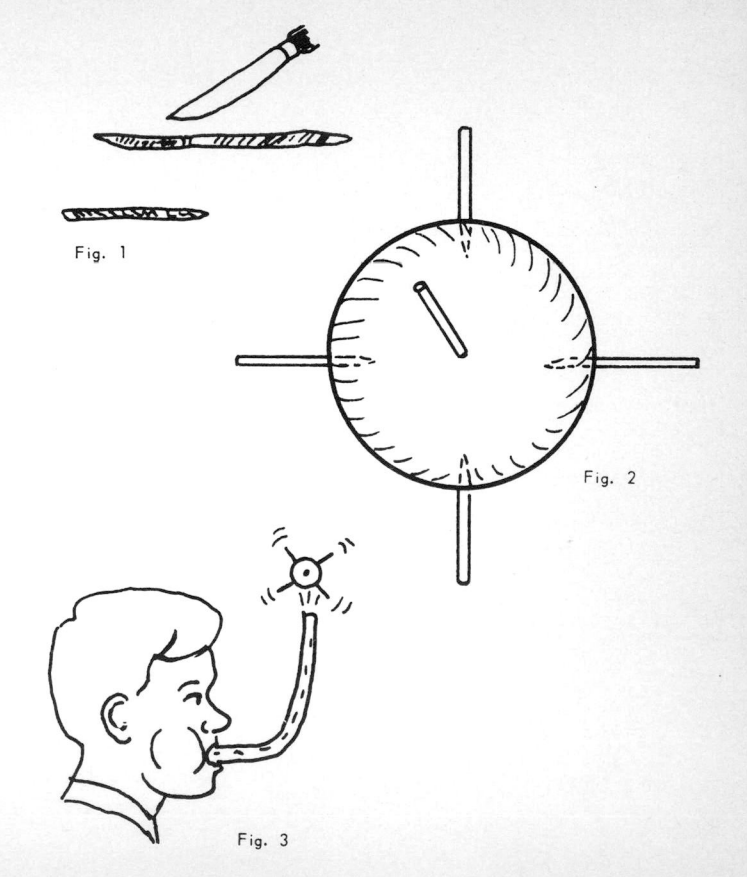

Fig. 1

Fig. 2

Fig. 3

average time required

30 minutes. If cotton is used instead of foam plastic, insert one toothpick through the center of the ball. It should protrude about ⅜ in. at both sides.

fish kite

materials and tools

Three sheets of wrapping tissue, newspaper, glue, four strings 15 in. long, crayons or paint, several strips of crepe paper or colored tissue paper ¼ by 10 in., ball of kite string.

procedure

1. Make a newspaper pattern of the fish without fins, about 30 in. long (Fig. 1).
2. Draw the mouth opening about 8 in. wide (Fig. 1).
3. Cut out two copies of the fish pattern from the tissue paper. Decorate and color as desired.
4. Make a pattern of the fins. Cut out two copies from the tissue and decorate (Fig. 2).
5. Glue the outside edges of the fish, attaching the fins between the sides of the fish as in Fig. 2. Do not glue the mouth.
6. Cut a strip of cardboard ¾ in. wide to fit around the inside of the fish's mouth. Overlap the cardboard, making a circular strip, and staple. Fit the cardboard circle inside the fish's mouth and glue or staple securely to the tissue paper (Fig. 3).
7. Fasten the four 15-in. strings to the cardboard equally spaced. Tie their loose ends together and attach them to the ball of string.

Fig. 1

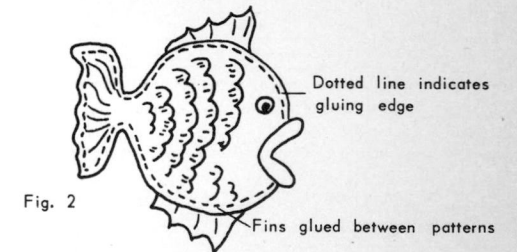

Dotted line indicates gluing edge

Fins glued between patterns

Fig. 2

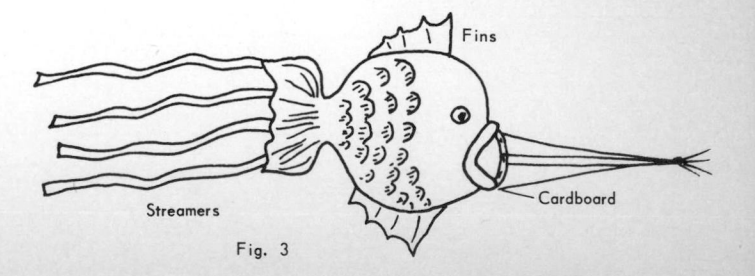

Fins

Streamers

Cardboard

Fig. 3

8. Attach short streamers to the tail (Fig. 3).

   To operate, pull through the air, allowing the kite to fill with air. As the wind pressure increases, slowly let out extra string until the kite is high in the air. Stop pulling the kite when the air currents are able to keep it aloft.

average time required

50 minutes. This project can be adapted for younger children if the leader prepares the patterns for the kite.

handy miniature scorekeeper

materials and tools

A piece of cardboard 3 by 5 in., sharp blade, four strips of light cardboard or heavy paper ⁷⁄₁₆ by 7 in., ink, glue or stapler.

procedure

1. With a razor blade or sharp knife, make eight ½-in. slits in the cardboard as shown in Fig. 1.
2. Starting 1 in. from the top of each strip, mark with ink at ½-in. intervals the numbers 0 to 9 (Fig. 2).
3. Thread the score tapes through the slits in the cardboard so that the numbers will show when the tape is moved forward or backward. Staple or glue together the ends of each tape to form a circle to the rear of the score card (Fig. 3). This little score box will tabulate up to a total of 99 points for each team.

average time required

50 minutes

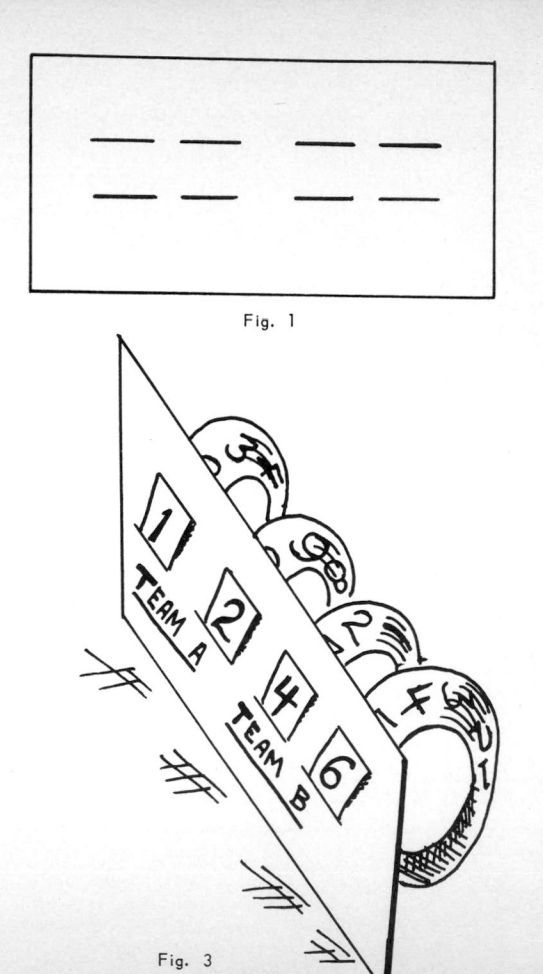

Fig. 1

Fig. 2

Fig. 3

hot pad

materials and tools

Heavy cotton yarn of various colors, about 20 ft. of strong string or cord, a piece of medium-heavy cardboard 7 by 6¾ in., weaving needle or bobby pin.

procedure

1. Mark off twenty-seven ¼-in. intervals at the top and bottom edges of the cardboard as shown in the illustration.
2. Cut a ⅛-in. slit at each marked interval.
3. To start the loom, tie a knot 3 in. from the end of the cord. Slide the cord into slit number 1 at the top of the cardboard. Pull the string through the cut in the loom until the knot is tight against the slit. Be sure the knot and the 3-in. tying piece are to the rear of the cardboard loom.
4. To thread the loom, bring the loom cord down the face of the cardboard to point A or to the first cut at the bottom of the cardboard. Run the string through slit A, then across the back of the cardboard to slit B. Bring cord out through cut B and up the face of the loom to slit number 2. Slide the cord through slit number 2. At this point, and using the 3-in. tying end, tie the two strings securely together. Bring the loom cord out through slit number 3 and down the face of the loom to slit C. Continue the above method to thread

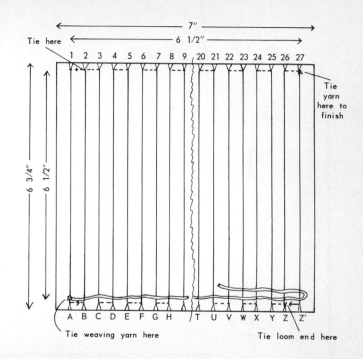

the loom completely. To fasten the final end of the loom cord, bring it back across the loom from slit Z' to slit Z and tie securely at this point.

5. Tie a piece of yarn to the loom cord at position A. Begin weaving by running the yarn over and under from left to right until you reach the right side of the loom. Change the direction of the weaving and return to the left side of the loom. Be sure that the over- and under-weaving is opposite the first crossing. Continue weaving back and forth across the loom until it is completely covered with yarn. To keep the yarn close together, push it tightly toward the bottom of the loom. By using several contrasting colors of yarn a beautiful pattern can be developed. To tie or finish, secure the end of the weaving yarn to the loom cord at position 27 at the top and rear of the loom.

6. To remove the hot pad from the cardboard frame, slip the top and bottom cord loops from their respective slits in the cardboard.

average time required

80 minutes. For variation, make the hot pad with such materials as twisted crepe-paper strips, narrow strips of cloth, or light-textured rope.

jitterbugs

materials and tools

Lightweight cardboard, strong cord.

procedure

1. On the cardboard, draw the body and leg designs of a man and a woman (Figs. 1 and 2).
2. Draw the arms (Figs. 3 and 4).
3. Cut out the body parts and punch holes through all points marked X. Assemble the parts by placing a short string through the matching holes and tying knots on the ends of the strings to prevent them from slipping through the holes (Fig. 5). Do not tie the joints too tightly.
4. Run a string through the two middle arm holes and tie the ends. Keep this string loose (Fig. 4).
5. Tie a 5-ft. length of string to the cord running between the two arms. Leave enough string hanging below the dancers to form an anchor. Dress and decorate the dancers as desired.
6. To manipulate, thumb-tack the end of the anchor string to the floor. Standing above the dancers, pull the string with little jerks, first tightening the string and then releasing it, causing the figures to dance.

155

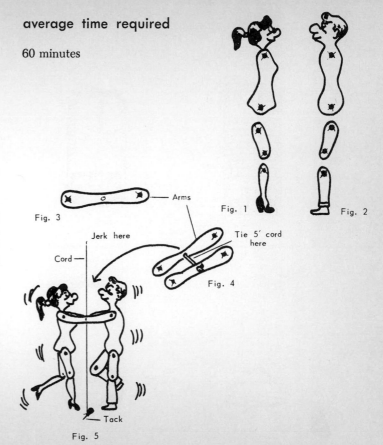

Fig. 3

Arms

Jerk here

Cord

Tie 5' cord here

Fig. 4

Fig. 1

Fig. 2

Tack

Fig. 5

lighthouse

materials and tools

Round cereal box, spool, hairpin or bobby pin, button, paints or crayons.

procedure

1. Three-fourths of an inch down from the top of the box, cut several evenly spaced windows about 1 by 1½ in. (Fig. 1).
2. To make the simulated light, place the button and then the spool on the hairpin. Punch a hole in the center of the box lid. On the underside of the lid, insert the hairpin ends through the hole. To hold the light securely in place, fold back the ends of the hairpin (Fig. 2).
3. At the bottom of the box, draw a door about 2½ by 1½ in. Cut on three sides and fold back (Fig. 3).
4. Place the lid on the box and decorate the lighthouse as desired (Fig. 4).
5. Twist the hairpin to make the light turn.

average time required

40 minutes

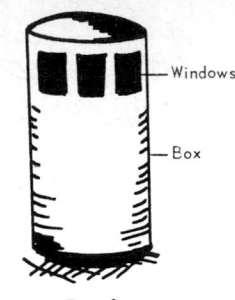

Windows

Box

Fig. 1

Light
Hole
Bobby pin
Box lid
Spool
Button

Fig. 2

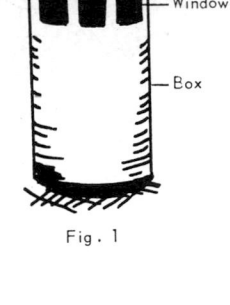

Fold

Door

Fig. 3

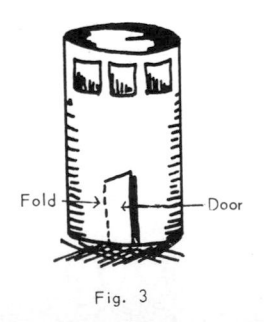

Decorated lighthouse

Fig. 4

log cabin

materials and tools

Magazines with large pages, a piece of heavy cardboard, eight 2-in. nails, strong glue, a piece of white construction paper, clothes hanger.

procedure

1. Cut the cardboard into a sheet 8 by 10 in. (Fig. 1).
2. Tear pages from a magazine and roll them into rods, or logs, about ¾ in. in diameter and in the different lengths needed. Glue the edges of the paper to prevent the log from unrolling (Fig. 2).
3. Push nails up through the cardboard at points marked X (Fig. 1). The shape of the cabin and the door positions can be changed by changing the positions of the upright nails.
4. Cut four logs 5 in. long and thread them on wires to form the roof arches as in Fig. 3.
5. Cut eight logs into 6-in. lengths and insert them upon the upright nails to form the framework of the house (Fig. 4).
6. To complete the framework, insert the wires protruding from the ends of the arches into the tops of the upright logs at the ends of the house. Set arches across 1 and 4 and across 7 and 8 (Fig. 4).

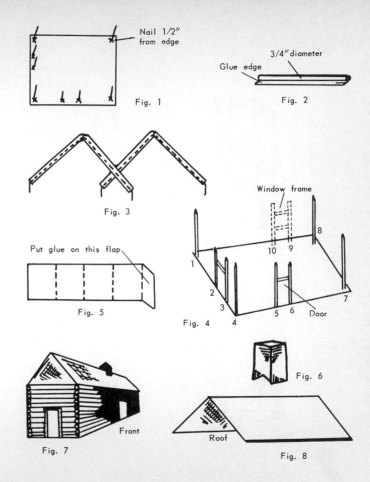

Nail 1/2" from edge

Fig. 1

3/4" diameter

Glue edge

Fig. 2

Fig. 3

Window frame

Put glue on this flap

Fig. 5

Fig. 4

Door

Fig. 6

Front

Fig. 7

Roof

Fig. 8

7. Cut logs to fit the dimensions of the house and put glue on the top and bottom edge of each log and set it in place. Finish the front and back ends of the house before putting on the sides. The logs on the front and back protrude beyond the edges of the frame. The side logs do not protrude, as shown in the illustration. Notice how the uprights between the front end and the sides, 2 and 3, brace the door logs. Open windows, placed at any desired position, can be made between upright logs. To make the top of the doors more secure, glue or wire a short piece of log at the top of the door opening between uprights 2 and 3, or 5 and 6. Windows can be braced with top and bottom logs between uprights 9 and 10 (Fig. 4).
8. Place roof logs on last. If you do not wish a log roof, use a folded piece of cardboard and glue it in place (Fig. 8).
9. From a piece of paper 3 by 4½ in. make a chimney. Make each side 1 in. wide and glue the extra ½-in. piece to hold the chimney together (Fig. 5). Hold the chimney at the rear of the house and below the arch, measure, and mark off the arch slant on the chimney box. Clip up the center of this arch and fold the clipped sides inward (Fig. 6). Put glue on these flaps and place the chimney over the roof. Hold it in place until the glue has set (Fig. 7).

average time required

120 minutes

paper-napkin holder

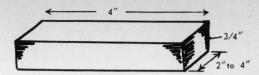

Fig. 1

materials and tools

Two metal lids from cottage cheese cartons or the ends of a tin can, one block of wood, paints, decals, pictures, steel wool, four small shingle nails, hammer.

procedure

1. Cut out a block of wood to the proper dimensions and sand it smooth. Sand in the direction of the grain (Fig. 1).
2. If you use can ends, cut them out with a can opener and rub the edges with steel wool to dull them and prevent metal slivers (Fig. 2).
3. Fasten both tin disks to the opposite sides of the block with nails. Bend the lower edge of the disks under the block or trim it off before nailing to the block (Fig. 3).
4. Decorate as desired and paint or stain the wood portion.

average time required

30 minutes

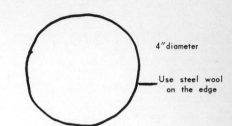

4" diameter

Use steel wool on the edge

Fig. 2

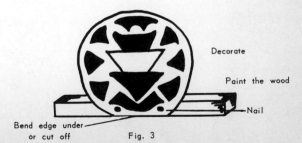

Decorate

Paint the wood

Nail

Bend edge under or cut off

Fig. 3

papier-mâché puppets or dolls

materials and tools

Newspapers, thin wheat paste, lightweight cardboard, two 12-in. pieces of string, poster paints or crayons, piece of crepe paper or cloth material 8 by 12 in.

procedure

1. To make the neck, cut out a piece of cardboard 4 by 6 in. Roll it into a tube with a diameter of about 1 in. and tie with a piece of string (Figs. 1 and 2).
2. Cut or tear twenty strips of newspaper about 1½ in. wide and twenty strips about ½ to 1 in. wide.
3. Hold all four corners of a full sheet of newspaper in one hand and wad it into a ball with the other hand (Fig. 3). This forms the base of the doll's head.
4. Wet one of the wider strips of paper with paste and wipe off the excess by pulling it through two fingers; then wrap it around the head. Continue adding paper strips until the base begins to take shape (Fig. 4).
5. Insert the four ends of left-over newspaper at the base of the head into the tube, or neck, and then wrap several strips crisscross over the head and down around the neck to anchor the head to the neck (Fig. 5).

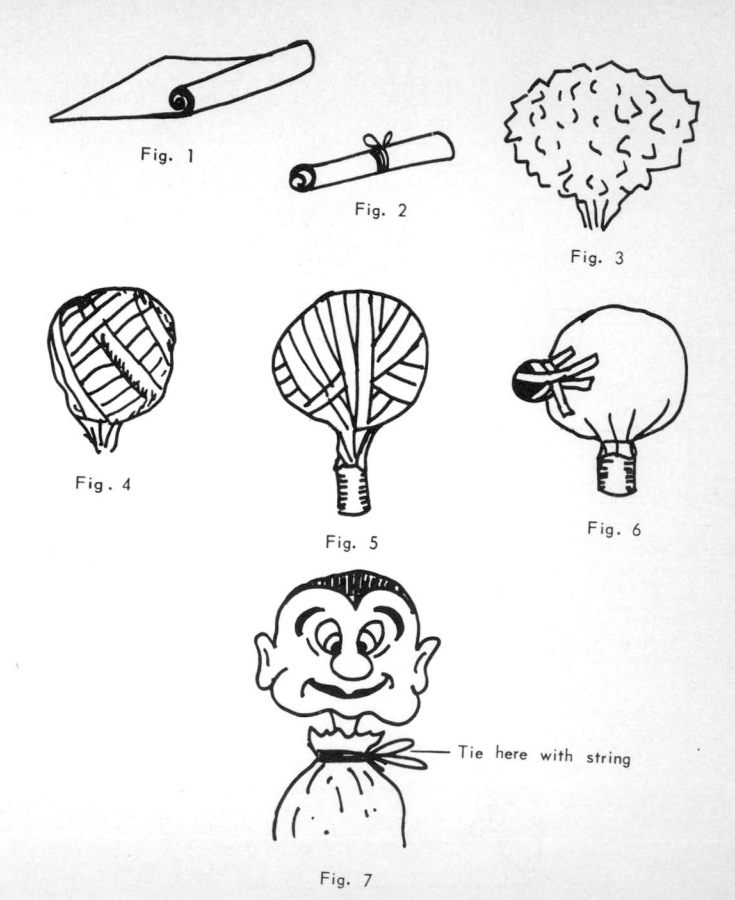

Fig. 1

Fig. 2

Fig. 3

Fig. 4

Fig. 5

Fig. 6

Tie here with string

Fig. 7

6. To form features such as cheeks, lips, nose, ears, eyebrows, and so forth, wad up the necessary amount of paper and saturate it with paste until it will mold almost like putty. Shape it and anchor it to the head with paper strips, using the crisscross method (Fig. 6). When making long features such as the ears of a rabbit, insert a popsicle stick, pencil, or a piece of wire and stick it in the head as a foundation. When the features have been completed stand the head, neck first, into a bottle or can and allow it to dry thoroughly before painting it. Do not lay it down to dry or one side of the head will flatten.
7. Paint with poster paint or color with crayons (Fig. 7).
8. Make a dress from cloth material or crepe paper by ruffling it about 1 in. down from the head and tying it with a piece of string or ribbon to hold it firmly to the neck (Fig. 7).

average time required

90 minutes, plus drying time.

pencil holder

materials and tools

The head section of an old automobile distributor, fast-drying enamel, piece of heavy cloth or felt.

procedure

1. Clean all the oil from the distributor head with soap and hot water. Enamel it a bright color.
2. Place the head upon a piece of felt and mark its size. Cut out the piece of felt and glue it to the bottom of the distributor to prevent it from scratching the finished surface of a table or desk.
3. Place on desk and insert pencils into the holes in the top of the distributor.

average time required

40 minutes. A piece of heavy blotter can be used in place of the felt. If neither is available, sand the bottom of the holder until smooth.

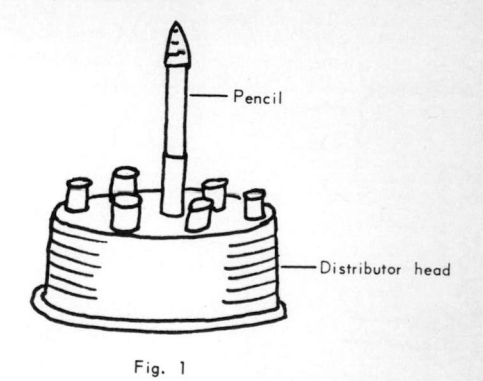

Pencil

Distributor head

Fig. 1

rope belt

materials and tools

A piece of ½-in. rope about 3 in. longer than needed to encircle your waist, cord, small block of wood ½ in. thick by 2 in. square.

procedure

1. With scissors taper the end of the rope and fold it, forming a 5-in. loop (Figs. 1 and 6). Wrap or lash it securely with strong cord, then cover with adhesive tape. If you lash the belt loop, do not use tape. To lash, fold a short piece of string and place it upon the belt loop as shown in Fig. 6. Hold the folded string in place and continue winding with the strong cord. Bind over the folded string until only a short loop protrudes at the end of the binding. Cut off the binding cord, leaving a short end. Thread the free end of the cord through the loop formed by the folded piece of string. Grasp the two ends of the folded string and pull on them. Pull the folded string from under the lashing cord, bringing the free end of the wrapping cord with it. This puts the end of the wrapping cord underneath itself and securely holds it in place. To finish, clip off the extra piece of wrapping string (Figs. 6 and 7).

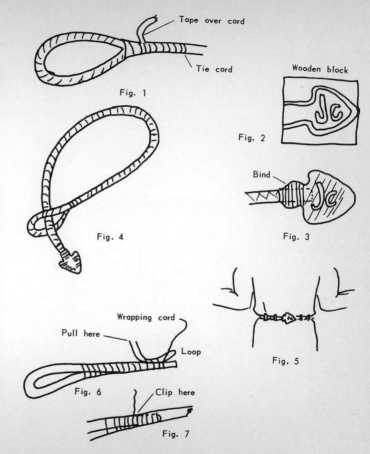

Tape over cord

Tie cord

Fig. 1

Wooden block

Fig. 2

Bind

Fig. 3

Fig. 4

Wrapping cord

Pull here

Loop

Fig. 6

Fig. 5

Clip here

Fig. 7

2. Carve the wooden buckle to any shape you wish, but be sure to make the sides wide and shaped to keep it from slipping out of the loop when the belt is buckled (Fig. 2). Decorate or initial the buckle.
3. Place the buckle on the rope and wrap it with cord or tape to hold it in place (Fig. 3).
4. To fasten the belt, place the loop over the carved block (Fig. 4).
5. Alternate buckles may be made from rocks, a notched stick, or a big button.

average time required

40 to 60 minutes, depending upon the type of buckle used.

rubber-headed drum

materials and tools

A round, one- or two-gallon ice cream carton or a two-pound coffee tin; a large, round-headed paper fastener; yarn; discarded tire tube; poster paint; knife; scissors; large needle; pencil; piece of cord about 40 in. long.

procedure

1. Remove lid and cut out the bottom of the carton. Color sides of the carton if desired (Fig. 4).
2. Push a large, round-headed paper fastener through the side of the carton as in Fig. 1, and tie the ends of the heavy cord just below the head of the fastener. This forms the loop that is to be placed around your neck to hold the drum while striking it. Be sure to spread the fastener inside the carton to hold it in place.
3. Place the end of the carton on the rubber tubing and draw a line around it. Cut out two rounds of rubber tubing ¼ in. larger than this pattern (Figs. 1 and 2).
4. Cut small ¼-in. slits around the rubber circles at 1½-in. intervals and ½ in. from the edge of the circle (Fig. 3).
5. Place the rubber circles at the ends of the carton and lace the yarn through the slits to hold them in place. Alternate

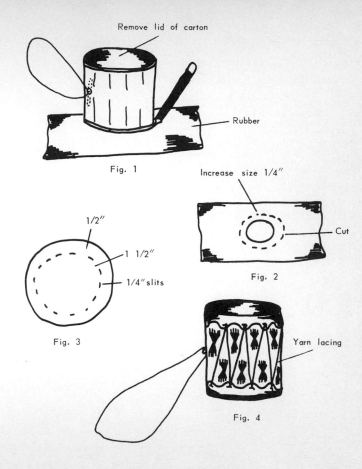

Remove lid of carton

Rubber

Fig. 1

Increase size 1/4"

Cut

Fig. 2

1/2"

1 1/2"

1/4" slits

Fig. 3

Yarn lacing

Fig. 4

the lacing from one rubber circle to the other and pull the yarn tightly to stretch the rubber circles over the drum head as tightly as possible. This will improve the tone of the drum (Fig. 4).

average time required

80 minutes

rustic picture frame

materials and tools

A small picture mounted on an 8-by-10-in. piece of dark paper, colored yarn, four straight ½-in.-thick wooden sticks cut from a tree, a sharp knife, thumbtacks, sandpaper.

procedure

1. Make two of the sticks 10 in. long and the other two 12 in. long. Trim the rough edges and notches and remove the bark, if desired. If you remove the bark, sand the sticks until smooth. Slightly point the ends of the sticks.
2. Place the ends of the sticks together as in Figs. 1 and 2 and, in crisscross fashion, tie them securely in place.
3. Turn the frame over and place the picture face down with its side edges resting upon the two side sticks. With thumbtacks fasten the picture in place (Fig. 2).
4. Turn the frame face up and hang it on the wall (Fig. 3).

average time required

40 minutes. To adapt this activity for older children have them notch the ends of each stick at the point at which they cross one another. Fit the sticks together at the notches for a smoother appearance.

167

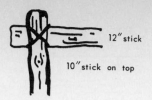

12" stick

10" stick on top

Fig. 1

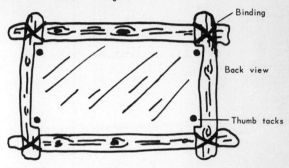

Binding

Back view

Thumb tacks

Fig. 2

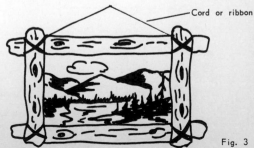

Cord or ribbon

Fig. 3

snapshot holder

materials and tools

A strip of leatherette or plastic automobile seat covering, heavy white paper, glue.

procedure

1. Measure the size of the snapshots to go in the folder and make the leatherette folder ¾ in. wider than the pictures. Make two slits ½ in. from the bottom of the folder and ½ in. apart. Follow the other measurements in the illustration to allow for folding and fastening (Fig. 1).
2. Cut out two strips of paper long enough to frame four pictures and to allow for the spaces between the pictures, as shown in Fig. 2.
3. Glue the two paper strips together at point A, then glue them to the leatherette folder (Fig. 3).
4. Fold the two strips of paper in accordion fashion and paste the pictures to the eight front and eight back sides. Fold the paper sections and cover with the leatherette holder. Insert the flap on the folder into the two slits to secure the cover (Fig. 4).

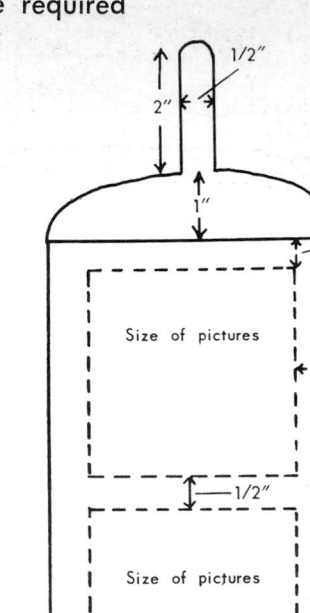

Fig. 1

168

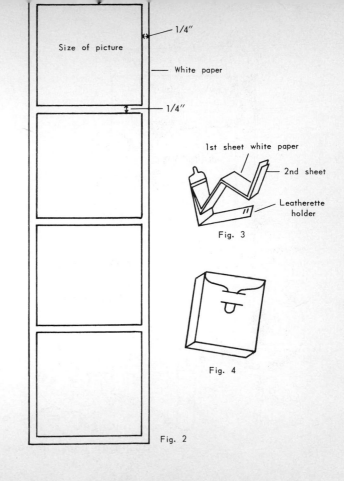

Size of picture

1/4″

White paper

1/4″

1st sheet white paper

2nd sheet

Leatherette holder

Fig. 3

Fig. 4

Fig. 2

spool animals

materials and tools

Construction paper or lightweight cardboard, glue, crayons, wooden spool, yarn or string.

procedure

1. Place the spool on end upon the paper and draw the circle of the spool. This will be the size of the animal's body. Draw the head and front legs of the animal, attached to the body circle (Fig. 1).
2. Repeat the same procedure as in Step 1 for the back of the animal's body. Attach a tail of yarn or string (Fig. 2).
3. Glue the front and back ends of the animal to the spool. Let dry before standing the animal on its legs (Fig. 3).

average time required

20 minutes

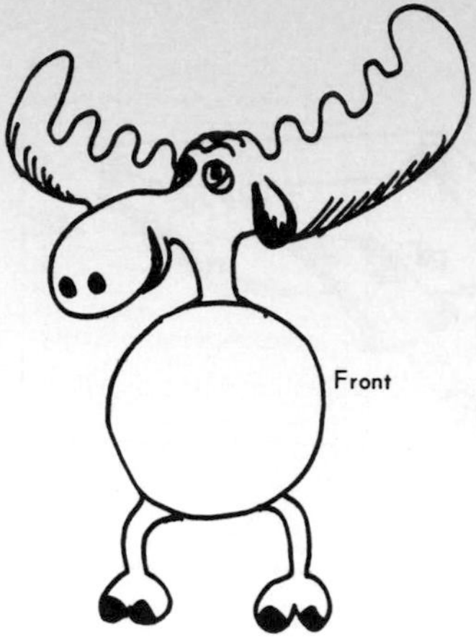

170

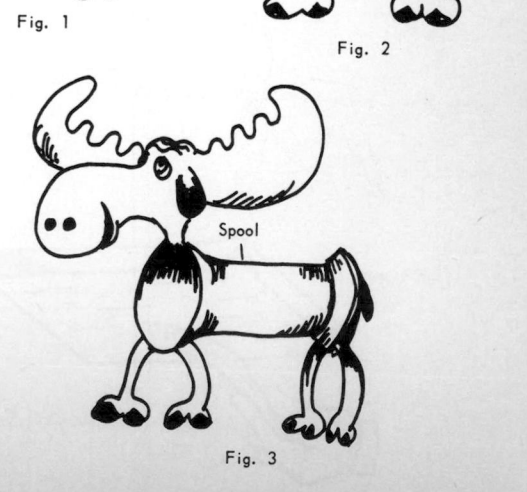

Front

Fig. 1

Back

Fig. 2

Spool

Fig. 3

spool penholder

materials and tools

Empty thread spool, a piece of wood about ½ in. thick by 3 in. square, fine sandpaper, glue, ink, varnish, small brush.

procedure

1. Sand the wooden base, rubbing with the grain until the edges, corners, and surfaces are smooth (Fig. 1).
2. Saw off one end of the spool at a 45° angle, leaving a portion of the round end intact (Fig. 2).
3. Glue the angle-cut edge of the spool to the center of the wood base (Fig. 3).
4. With ink, place the name or initials of the owner upon the wooden platform (Fig. 3).
5. Stain the penholder and base (Fig. 3).

average time required

60 minutes

Sand with grain

Fig. 1

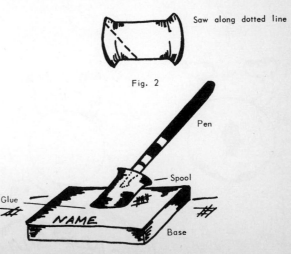

Saw along dotted line

Fig. 2

Pen

Spool

Glue

NAME

Base

Fig. 3

sword pins

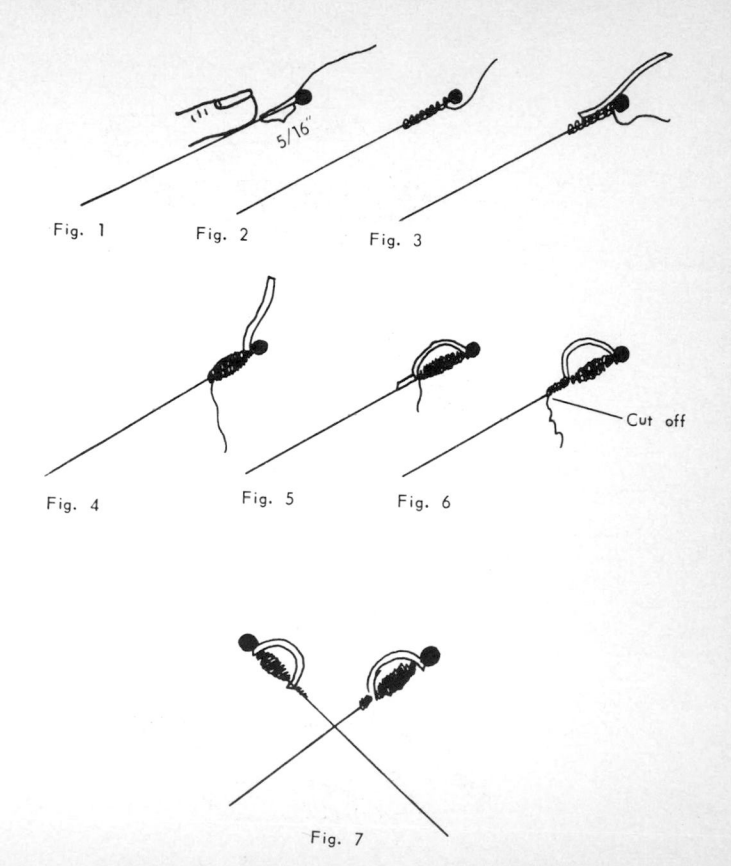

Fig. 1 Fig. 2 Fig. 3

Fig. 4 Fig. 5 Fig. 6 Cut off

Fig. 7

materials and tools

Two corsage pins about 1½ to 2 in. long, two pieces of boondoggle 1½ in. long, black sewing thread (medium weight), shellac or glue.

procedure

1. Insert the pin into a piece of flat scrap wood to hold it steady and wrap the upper section near the head of the pin with thread. Cover about ½ in. of the pin with a thin layer of thread. To start wrapping, place the end of the thread on the pin and hold it in place with the tip of your left index finger. Holding the spool in your right hand, wrap the thread around the pin several times, then wrap back over the first wraps to hold the thread in place (Figs. 1 and 2).
2. Hold the thread tightly and set in place with glue or shellac. Let dry (Fig. 2).
3. Place a strip of boondoggle along the top edge of the pin, shiny side down, extending above the pin head (Fig. 3).
4. Hold the boondoggle in place and begin wrapping the thread around the pin, bringing your wrapping up and over the section of boondoggle. Continue wrapping the thread

back and forth over the boondoggle until the sword handle resembles a cigar shape. Be sure to finish the wrapping at the bottom of the sword handle (Fig. 4).

5. Fold the loose end of the boondoggle back over the wrapped section, leaving it loose and rounded as a hand guard on a sword. Hold it in place and again start wrapping with the thread over the bottom end of the boondoggle guard. Wrap the boondoggle securely in place, then seal the thread in place with shellac or glue. When it is dry, cut off the extra thread (Figs. 5 and 6).

6. Make two swords and pin them crosswise on a shirt or dress (Fig. 7).

average time required

40 minutes

table croquet

materials and tools

Two small spools, four to six checkers or differently colored small marbles, sheet of plastic foam about ½ in. thick, ten 5-in. long pieces of wire.

procedure

1. Cut the foam into twenty 1½-in. squares (Fig. 1).
2. Bend the wires into the shape of an arch. Insert the ends of the wires into the foam squares (Fig. 2).
3. Cut off one rim from each spool. The spools serve as posts in the game (Fig. 3).
4. Color each checker a different color or use colored marbles. These are used in place of balls. Instead of a mallet, use the thumb and first or second finger to flip the checkers or marbles (Fig. 4).
5. Place the arches upon a flat table surface as in croquet and use regular croquet rules when playing the game.

average time required

40 minutes

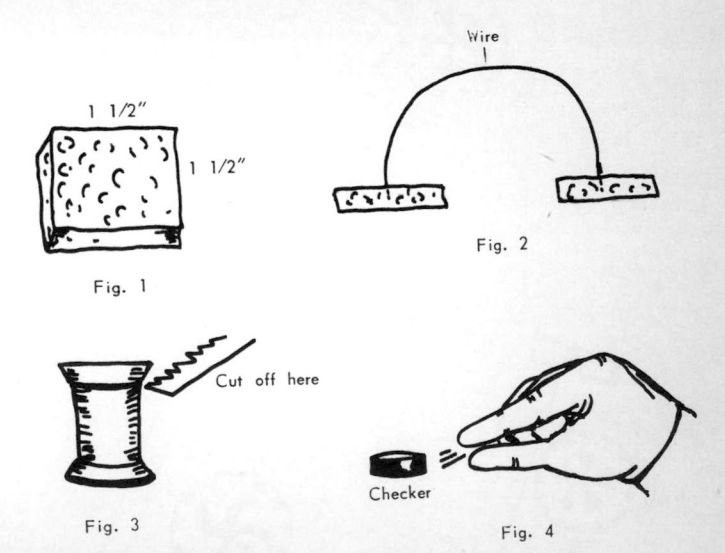

1 1/2"

1 1/2"

Fig. 1

Wire

Fig. 2

Cut off here

Fig. 3

Checker

Fig. 4

wheel runner

materials and tools

One wheel with a diameter of 6 in. or more, a flat piece of wood about 30 in. long by 3 in. wide, a piece of wood 6 by 3 in., nails, hammer.

procedure

1. Nail the short piece of wood on the end of the long stick. Bend the nails and hammer them down flat on the wrong side to secure them (Fig. 1).
2. To operate, hold the stick in the right hand and the wheel in the left hand and roll the wheel down the stick to start it (Fig. 2). Keep the wheel moving by running forward and at the same time pushing the wheel forward with the cross bar. The wheel is guided by turning the stick right or left as desired (Fig. 3).

average time required

15 minutes. The wheel can be decorated with colored or tissue paper. Lace the paper between the spokes to form designs.

175

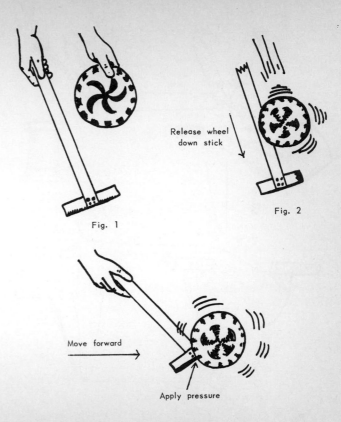

Fig. 1

Release wheel down stick

Fig. 2

Move forward

Apply pressure

wrapped wire or rod figures

materials and tools

Clothes hangers or wire, magazines or yarn, glue, wire cutters, pliers.

procedure

1. Draw a stick diagram of the figure you wish to make. Use your imagination and create something unusual (Fig. 1).
2. Cut the hanger wire into the sizes and number of pieces you will need. The fewer pieces, the better. It is easier to bend than to piece together (Fig. 2).
3. Bend the wire above the head to form ears (Fig. 2).
4. Cut paper from a magazine, roll it about ½ in. thick, glue together, then slip it over the body, head, and tail wires (Fig. 3).
5. Wrap the leg wires in place and slide on the paper rolls. Bend the short protruding ends of the wires to hold the paper rolls in place (Fig. 3).

average time required

90 minutes. Optional—wrap the wire with yarn.

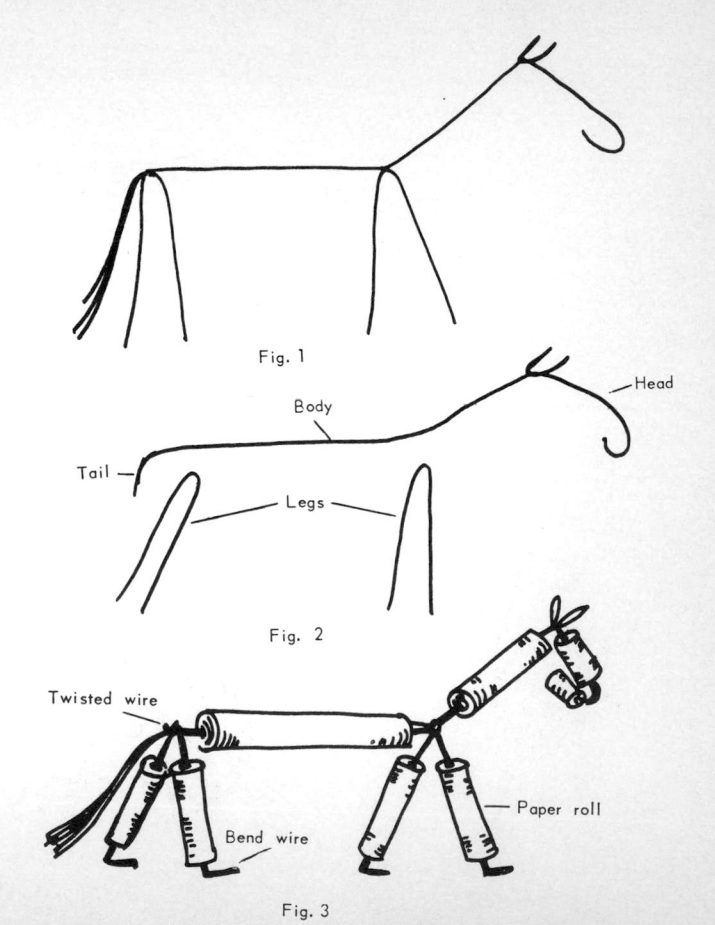

Fig. 1

Body

Head

Tail

Legs

Fig. 2

Twisted wire

Paper roll

Bend wire

Fig. 3

part five   fifth-grade ages

fifth-grade ages

Black Walnut Belt or Hatband 179

Carton Hats 181

Christmas Wreath 182

Clothes-hanger Bookend 184

Crayon Stenciling 185

Crazy-quilt Vase 186

Fluffy-paper Vase 187

Flying Propeller 188

Girl's Wrist Purse 189

Glass Inking 190

Handy Pants Hanger 191

Inlaid Checkerboard 192

Inlaid Serving Tray 193

Jack-in-the-box 194

Matching Dolls 196

Moving Flip-top Faces 198

Painted Drinking Glass 199

Papier-mâché Piggy Bank 200

Peek-a-vue 202

See Seeds Grow 203

Simple String Chain 204

Soap Carving 205

Spool Dolls 206

Tie Rack 207

Twisted-crepe-paper Vase 208

Wriggly Dragon 209

black walnut belt or hatband

materials and tools

Several dried black walnuts, strong cord or narrow leather strips or ribbon, a vise and a fine blade saw or a jig saw, paraffin wax or brown shoe polish.

procedure

1. Place a dried walnut into the vise and saw it crosswise into several sections. Continue making sections until you have enough to make the belt or band.
2. With a sharp instrument clean the meat from the disks.
3. Separate the disks according to size. It is usually best to make belts and bands from nut disks that are approximately the same size.
4. Cut two lengths of cord 10 in. longer than the required belt length. Tie the cords together at one end. Be sure to make this knot about 5 in. above the ends of the cord. The 5 in. are for tying the belt around your waist (Fig. 1).
5. Place the nut sections in the positions desired and lace them together with the cord (Figs. 1 and 2).
6. When the belt is finished, tie the remaining cord ends into a knot. At each end of the belt you should have two 5-in. lengths of cord to be used to tie the belt around your waist (Fig. 2).

179

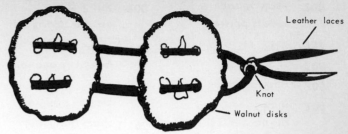

Leather laces

Knot

Walnut disks

Fig. 1

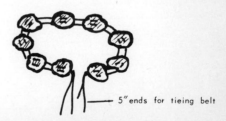

5" ends for tieing belt

Fig. 2

7. Rub each walnut section with brown shoe polish or with paraffin wax. Highly polish the sections with a dry cloth.

average time required

If the disks are prepared for the children, the stringing and polishing will take about 40 minutes. If not, the time required will depend upon the length of the band or belt and the availability of tools.

carton hats

materials and tools

Ice cream carton, glue, cardboard, crayons or poster paints, other desired decorations, scissors.

procedure

1. Draw a line around the carton 2 in. from the bottom or open end (Fig. 1).
2. Draw lines at uneven intervals from the open end of the carton to the line drawn above it. Cut the lines like a fringe (Fig. 1). Fold the fringed flaps straight out (Fig. 2).
3. Cut a brim from a piece of cardboard. To obtain the desired size for the brim, place the hat on paper and draw the pattern desired (Fig. 3). Cut out the brim and glue it to the clipped edges. Be sure the clipped edges are underneath the brim (Fig. 4).
4. Decorate as desired.

average time required

40 minutes. One can make hats ranging from top hats to caps by changing height of crown and shape of brim.

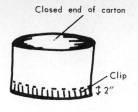
Closed end of carton
Clip
2"

Fig. 1

Fig. 2

Fig. 3

Fig. 4

christmas wreath

materials and tools

Clothes hanger, wire (flexible florist's wire is best), greenery from shrubs or evergreens cut into 5- or 6-in. lengths, green or red ribbon 3 in. wide (plastic is best for outdoors), cones—painted or natural.

procedure

1. Grasp the hanger at its ends and with steady pressure force it into a circle. Do not untwist or separate the top of the hanger (Fig. 1).
2. Take about five green twigs and, holding their ends together, place them at the top of the hanger as shown in Fig. 1. Using lightweight wire, wrap the green twig ends tightly to the hanger. Make an extra wrap of wire around the body of the greens to catch and hold the loose ends.
3. Take the same number of green twigs and place them on the hanger in the same direction as the first, covering the exposed wired ends by overlapping. Loop wire around the second twigs, securing them tightly to the hanger as in Fig. 2.
4. Continue all the way around the hanger until you reach the starting point. Tuck the ends of the last bunch of greenery under the first bunch and wire securely.

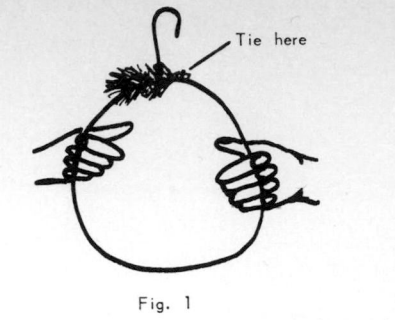

Tie here

Fig. 1

Fig. 2

Fig. 3

5. Cones, ribbons, and Christmas ornaments may be added to complete the wreath (Fig. 3).

average time required

60 minutes

clothes-hanger bookend

Fig. 1

Fig. 2

Fig. 3

materials and tools

Clothes hanger, piece of felt or cardboard, glue or tape, hammer, boondoggle, ribbon or yarn, buttons, colored inks, crayons, any other desired decorations.

procedure

1. Take a wire clothes hanger and straighten it out into an oblong shape (Fig. 1). A hammer may be needed to straighten the wire.
2. Bend both ends up so that they are about parallel and form right angles with the middle section. Bend the hook slightly down (Fig. 2).
3. Wrap the entire clothes hanger, with the exception of the hook, with boondoggle, yarn, or ribbon (Fig. 3).
4. Draw the desired face and tail design on the felt or cardboard. Cut them out and decorate the parts with buttons, yarn, and so forth (Fig. 4).
5. Glue or sew the head and tail at the position required (Figs. 4 and 5).

Fig. 4

Head

Tail

average time required

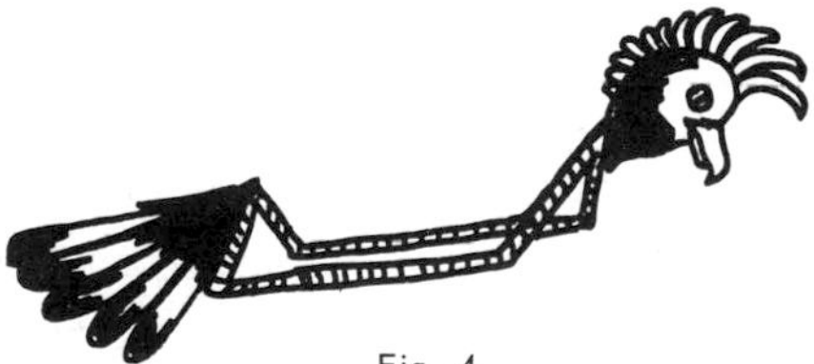

60 minutes

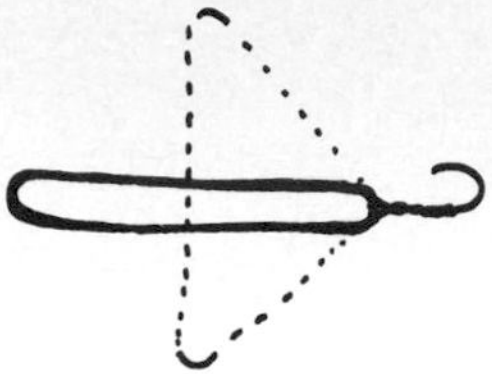

Fig. 5

crayon stenciling

materials and tools

Dish towel, carbon paper, crayons, iron, wax paper.

procedure

1. Select a design or picture you wish to stencil on the dish towel. Place the carbon face down on the material. Over this set the pattern. Trace this pattern on the cloth (Fig. 1).
2. Remove the pattern and carbon paper and color the design with crayons.
3. Place a piece of wax paper on the ironing board. Put the pattern face down on the wax paper. Press with hot iron on the wrong side of the towel. Press until the design comes through the material. Do not wash material for several days after stenciling.

average time required

40 minutes

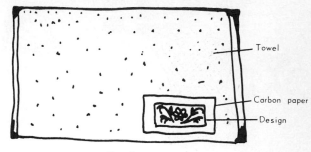

Fig. 1

crazy-quilt vase

materials and tools

Vase-shaped bottle, such as a plastic liquid detergent bottle with its neck trimmed off, old magazine (for colored pictures), shellac, paint brush, glue.

procedure

1. Cut colored pictures into small pieces.
2. Put glue on back of each piece of paper and place on the jar in a crazy-quilt pattern. Trim edges and fit pieces in without overlapping. Cover the entire jar (Fig. 1).
3. The rim of the vase may be cut off, painted gold, or covered with paper pieces (Fig. 2).
4. After the vase is completed, shellac and let dry.

average time required

80 minutes

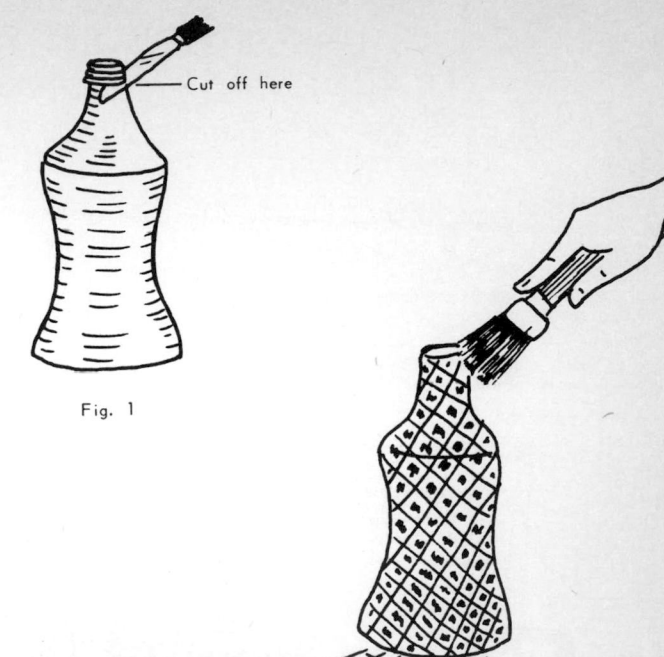

— Cut off here

Fig. 1

Fig. 2

fluffy-paper vase

materials and tools

Colored tissue paper or crepe paper, a new eraser-tipped pencil, paste or glue, a vase-shaped bottle.

procedure

1. Cut tissue paper into many 1-in. squares.
2. Cover a small section of the bottle with paste (Fig. 1).
3. Press the four corners of each small tissue paper square around the eraser end of the pencil and press it into place on the bottle close together to give a pile effect. If you do not use a pencil to place the squares, press them into position with the little finger. Do not put tissue on the bottom of the vase (Fig. 2). To obtain a fluffier cover, place a square of material between your fingers and as you press it into place upon the bottle, turn your fingers and twist the paper slightly.

average time required

30 to 90 minutes, or longer, depending on the complexity of the design.

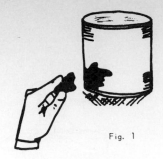

Fig. 1

Fig. 2

flying propeller

materials and tools

Spool, two small nails, one large nail, one tin-can top, string, pliers, tin cutters, hammer.

procedure

1. Draw a propeller on the tin-can top and cut it out. Cover the propeller edges with tape to prevent edges from cutting. Make two holes the size of the small nails in the center of the propeller (Fig. 1).
2. Nail the two small nails into the top of the spool to correspond with the two holes in the center of the propeller, then cut off the heads of the nails (Fig. 2).
3. Wrap the string around the spool and slip the spool onto the large nail (Fig. 3).
4. Holding the propeller blades between the thumbs and fingers of both hands, twist or bend the ends of the propeller slightly right and left, or opposite to one another. Place the propeller over the two small nails (Fig. 3).
5. Hold the nail and spool as in Fig. 4 and pull the string sharply, letting the spool spin on the nail. At the same time, quickly raise or push upward the hand holding the nail. This upward action of the hand and the spinning of the spool throws the propeller into flight. The propeller, if properly balanced, will fly high into space.

Positions of nails and holes in top of propellor should coincide

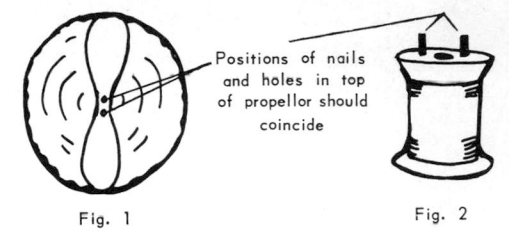

Fig. 1   Fig. 2

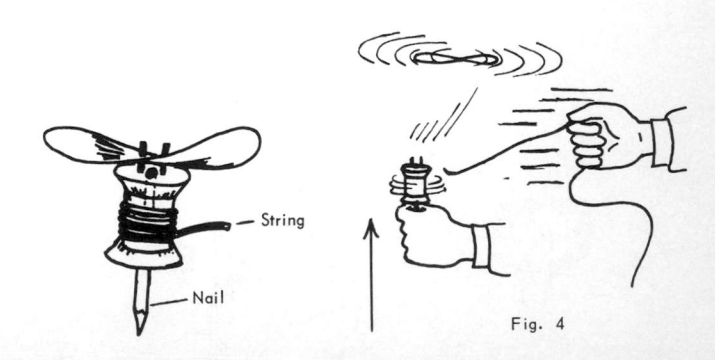

String

Nail

Fig. 3   Fig. 4

girl's wrist purse

materials and tools

Piece of rubber inner tube or plastic automobile seat cover material, two buttons, plastic lacing or yarn, needle and thread.

procedure

1. Draw diagram on the piece of rubber inner tube or plastic and cut out. Cut slits and sew button as illustrated (Fig. 1).
2. Cut out wrist band ¾ in. wide and long enough to fit wrist. Sew a button on one end of the band and make a ½-in. slit buttonhole at the other end (Fig. 2).
3. Fold purse and sew sides together with plastic lacing or yarn (Fig. 3).
4. Slide strap through slits and place around the wrist and fasten (Fig. 3).
5. To button down flap, first fold front flap A to inside. This flap prevents money from slipping from purse. Next fold flap B down over the front of the purse and button it securely (Fig. 4).

average time required

60 minutes

189

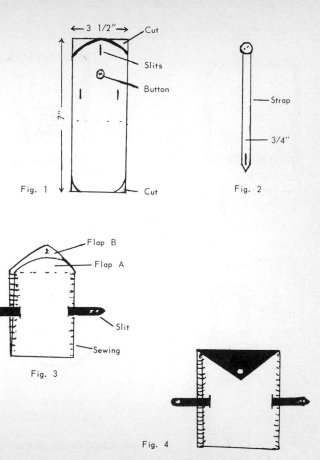

Fig. 1

Fig. 2

Fig. 3

Fig. 4

glass inking

materials and tools

A piece of clear window glass, black masking tape, aluminum foil, black India ink, a picture or design, cardboard, yarn, fine pen.

procedure

1. Select a picture or design you wish to ink onto the glass. Place design face down on glass and secure it with masking tape (Fig. 1).
2. Turn glass over and trace picture on the glass with ink (Fig. 2). Best results are obtained by using a daubing or light tapping action.
3. Let the finished picture dry for a few minutes and then remove the picture from the back of the glass. Turn the glass over so that the inked side is down and now becomes the back of the glass. Cut out a piece of foil and a piece of cardboard to fit the back of the glass and lay the shiny side of the foil next to the inked surface. Place the piece of cardboard next to the foil and tape it securely to the glass by lapping the tape over the cardboard and onto the glass. The black tape running around the glass forms a frame for the picture (Figs. 3 and 4).
4. To make the picture hanger, use masking tape to secure a short piece of yarn to the back of the picture (Fig. 4).

average time required

60 minutes or more depending on the complexity of the design. Colored ink may also be used.

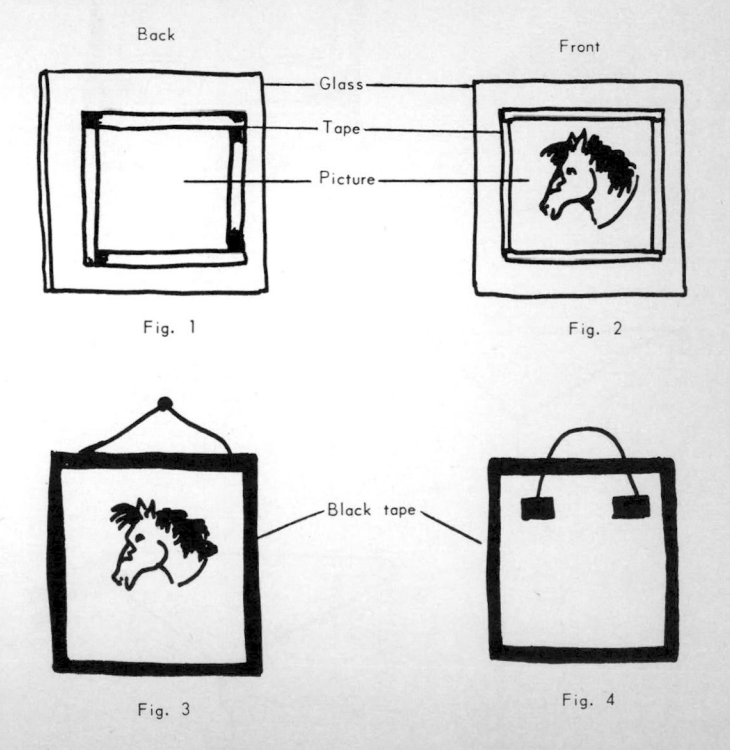

Fig. 1

Fig. 2

Fig. 3

Fig. 4

handy pants hanger

materials and tools

One clothes hanger, pliers.

procedure

1. Place the pliers at point A at the end of the hanger and twist up. Do this at both ends to form the loops (Fig. 1).
2. Place the pliers at point B and twist pliers to form the square corner at B (Figs. 2 and 3).
3. If the end loops do not stand upright, place the pliers inside the loop and twist it into the position desired (Fig. 3).
4. Hang the pants by the belt loops.

average time required

15 minutes. If desired the hanger can be wrapped with yarn. Wrapping time will be about 40 minutes.

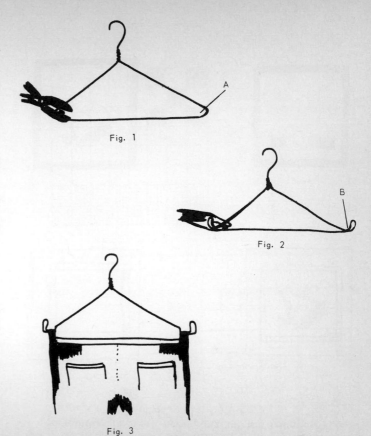

Fig. 1

Fig. 2

Fig. 3

inlaid checkerboard

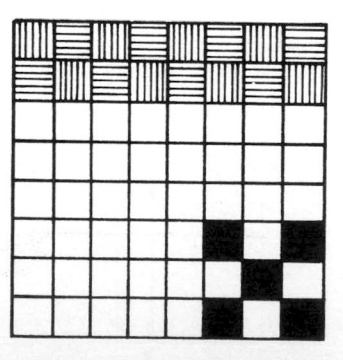

Fig. 1

materials and tools

Square of ¼-in. plywood, 12 by 12 in., one box of round applicator sticks, razor blade, Dupont glue, dark stain or ink, ruler, pencil.

procedure

1. Around the edge of the board mark off 1½-in. sections and draw lines across the board connecting these marks to form 1½-in. squares (Fig. 1).
2. Cut the slender wooden applicators into lengths 1½ in. long.
3. Smear glue on the first square in the top row and place the wooden rounds parallel to one another and across the square until the square is covered.
4. Proceed with the next square but place the rounds up and down instead of across. This change of direction sets off each square. Rows one and two are completed as in Fig. 2.
5. Continue alternating rounds on the squares until the checkerboard is completed.
6. Stain or ink all the squares in which the rounds are running in the same direction, that is, every other square. (See lower right-hand corner in Fig. 2.) This board makes a suitable gift for any checker or chess player.

Fig. 2

inlaid serving tray

materials and tools

A box of round or flat wood applicator sticks, glue, a piece of ¼-in. plywood, stain or varnish, pencil, razor blade, small handles (purchased from hardware store). Rope, leather strips, or heavy yarn may also be used for the handles.

procedure

1. Decide on a pattern and draw it on the plywood with pencil. The easiest designs are composed of squares or triangles (Fig. 1).
2. Cut the sticks into the desired sizes and, following the pattern, glue the sticks in place. Refer to the project "Inlaid Checkerboard" (Fig. 2).
3. Varnish or stain the entire board one color. If you wish to make different colored sections, paint them with India ink before applying the varnish.
4. Place handles at the ends of the tray (Fig. 2).

average time required

60 to 180 minutes, depending on the size of the tray and the complexity of the design.

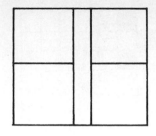

Fig. 1

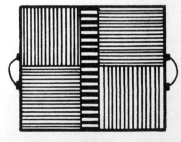

Fig. 2

jack-in-the-box

materials and tools

A clean ice cream or cottage cheese carton, four elastic bands, cardboard, four paper fasteners, a spool doll or any similar object that has an over-all length of about 3½ in.

procedure

1. Cut from the cardboard a disk that has a diameter 1 in. less than the bottom of the carton (Fig. 1).
2. Approximately ½ in. from the edge, cut four small slits evenly spaced around the disk (Fig. 1).
3. Thread two elastic bands down through slit A and bring them across the disk and up through slit C. Similarly, thread two elastic bands through slits B and D (Fig. 1).
4. Spread the paper fasteners slightly and place them on the elastic bands (Fig. 1).
5. Punch four holes corresponding to the slits in the disk in the sides of the carton about 1 in. from the top edge (Fig. 2).
6. Place the disk in the box and push the pointed ends of the fasteners through the side holes. Spread the ends of the fasteners on the outside of the box to prevent them from slipping back into the carton. This forms a platform on which to rest the jumping jack (Fig. 2).

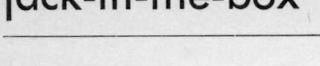

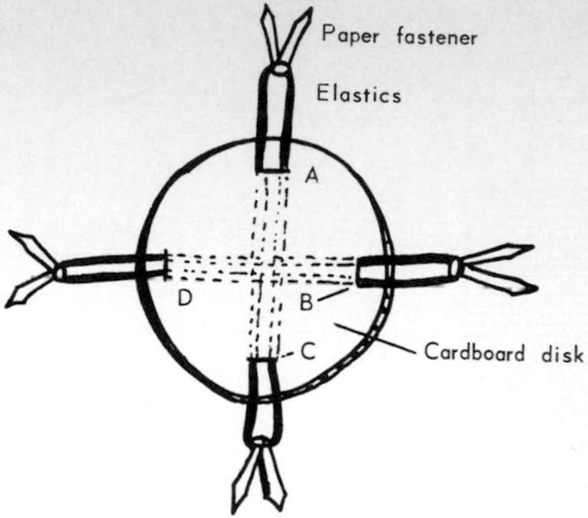

Paper fastener
Elastics
A
D B
C
Cardboard disk

Fig. 1

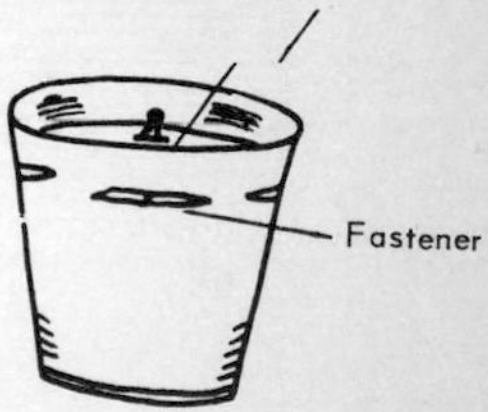

Disk
Fastener

Fig. 2

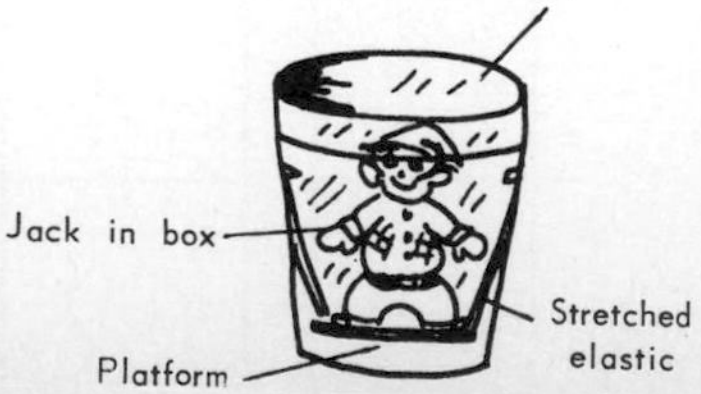

Lid
Jack in box
Stretched elastic
Platform

Fig. 3

Fig. 4

7. Decorate the outside of the box with pictures or brightly colored designs.
8. To operate, place the doll on the platform and push it down into the box until the lid of the box can be put into place. When the lid is removed the jack will jump from the box.

average time required

60 to 80 minutes. This project makes a wonderful gift for a younger brother or sister.

matching dolls

materials and tools

Yarn, boondoggle, strips of cloth, cardboard, narrow ribbon.

procedure

1. Cut out a piece of cardboard 7½ by 5 in. (Fig. 1).
2. Wrap yarn, boondoggle, or strips of cloth about twenty times lengthwise around the cardboard. Slip a piece of string under the wrapping at one end and tie a knot in it (Fig. 2). Slide scissors under the other (bottom) end and cut the material. Remove the lengths of material from the cardboard (Fig. 3).
3. To form the doll's head tie a piece of string about 1½ in. from the top of the material. If desired, cut a round piece of cloth with a 4-in. diameter. Fold it over the doll's head and tie in place with a piece of yarn (Fig. 4).
4. Wrap the yarn or other material from ten to twenty times crosswise around the cardboard frame (Fig. 1).
5. Slide the wrapping from the frame and tie a string around the material about 1 in. from each end (Fig. 5).
6. Slip the above wrapping through the center of the body to form the arms. Tie a piece of ribbon around the doll's body, directly below the arms, to form the waist. Clip the material at the ends of the arms to resemble hands, or leave unclipped if desired. You may cover each hand with a piece

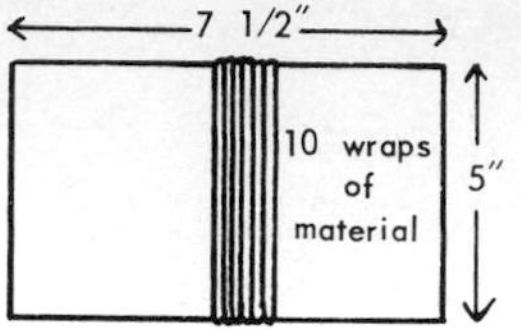

Fig. 1

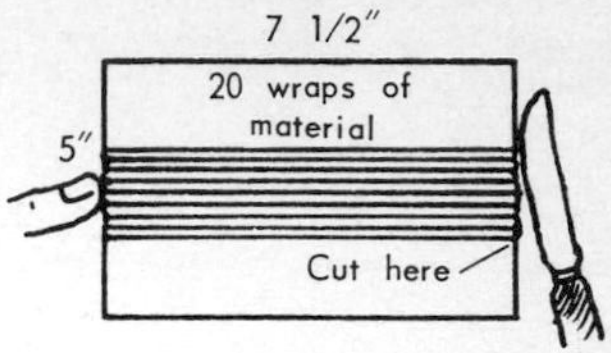

Fig. 2

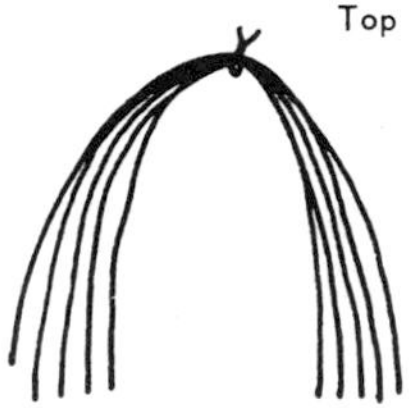

Fig. 3

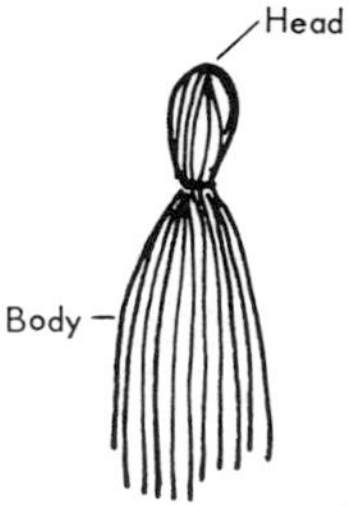

Fig. 4

Fig. 5

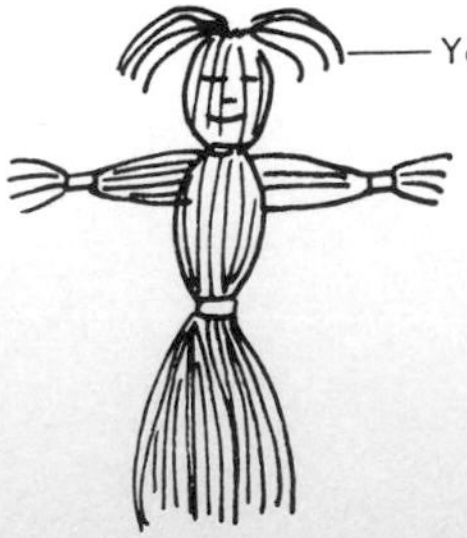

Fig. 6

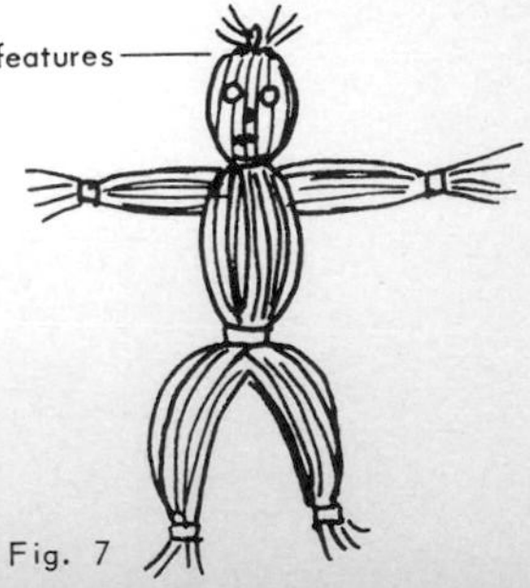

Fig. 7

of cloth. The features may be sewed on with colored yarn or thread. Buttons and other decorations make good eyes (Fig. 6). This is a girl doll.

7. To make a boy doll, divide the material at the bottom below the waist and tie each leg with a piece of string. You may clip the feet or cover with a piece of cloth (Fig. 7).

average time required

40 minutes. The prettiest dolls are made with narrow strips of brightly colored cloth materials. When using cloth, cut down the number of times the material is wrapped around the frame or make the frame bigger to make the doll larger. The small yarn or boondoggle dolls can be pinned to your coat. The larger cloth dolls can be used as toys or used to decorate a girl's dressing table or bed.

moving flip-top faces

materials and tools

One cigarette flip-top box, one matchstick, glue, colored paper, an elastic band, yarn or any other type of decoration desired, small piece of string.

procedure

1. Punch two holes in one side of the box. Make one hole in the top section and the second hole in the lower part of the box. If possible, tie the elastic band so that the knot is on the inside of the box (Fig. 1).
2. Punch a hole through the top of the box. Thread the two ends of string down through this hole, leaving the string with a loop in it about half way down the back of the box on the outside. Now on the inside of the flap, tie the string in a firm knot. Place a broken matchstick between the knot and the hole for support (Fig. 2).
3. Using this box as the foundation, create any type character you wish. The lid opening should be used to form the mouth (Fig. 3).
4. To open and shut the mouth, hold the box between thumb and third finger. Place your index finger in the loop and work it up and down.

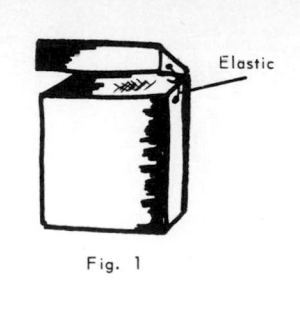

Elastic

Fig. 1

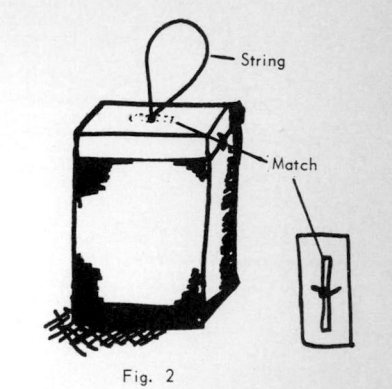

String

Match

Fig. 2

Fig. 3

198

painted drinking glass

materials and tools

Drinking glass, design, quick-drying enamel, paint, brush, paste.

procedure

1. Cut out design and paste it to the inside of the glass (Fig. 1).
2. Following the pattern, paint the design on the outside of the glass (Fig. 2).
3. Let the paint dry thoroughly on the glass before removing the pattern. (Do not wash the glass for a few hours or the paint may smear.)
4. If you wish to use more than one color in your design, let the first color dry completely before using another color.

average time required

40 minutes or more, depending upon the complexity of the design.

Design glued to inside of glass

Apply paint to outside of glass

Fig. 1

Painted glass with pattern removed

Fig. 2

199

papier-mâché piggy bank

materials and tools

A long or small rubber balloon, newspaper, thin wallpaper or wheat paste, poster paint or quick-drying enamel, heavy cord or light rope.

procedure

1. Blow the balloon full of air and tie with cord to prevent the air from escaping. Let the cord ends hang—do not cut them off (Fig. 1).
2. Fill a small bowl with thinned wheat paste or wallpaper paste.
3. Cut or tear strips of newspaper ½ to 1½ in. wide.
4. Dip strips of paper in paste; as you remove the strips draw them between two fingers to wipe off most of the paste.
5. Wrap the wet strip around the balloon. Continue until you have several layers of paper ⅛ in. thick or more on the balloon. Leave the cord dangling at the rear of the pig's body (Fig. 2).
6. Make a ball of paper, soak it in the paste, and mold a head. Place the head on the balloon body and fasten it securely by using strips of papier-mâché as you would use tape (Fig. 3).

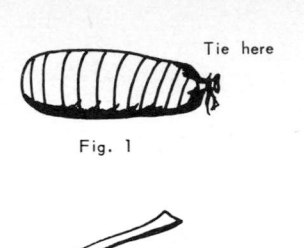

Tie here

Fig. 1

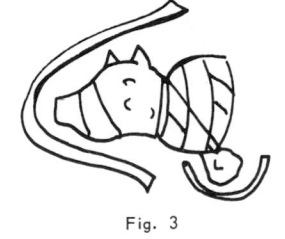

Fig. 3

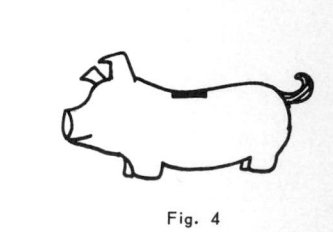

Fig. 2

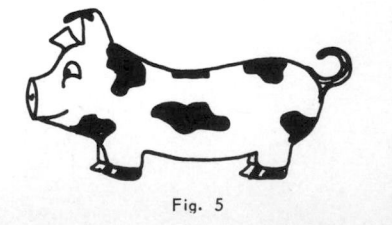

Fig. 4

Fig. 5

7. Let the pig dry for several days and then cut a slit in the top of the body for the money slot. Be sure to puncture the balloon (Fig. 4).
8. Color as desired. Wax and curl the loose cord ends to form the pig's tail (Fig. 5).

average time required

80 minutes of working time plus the time required to dry.

peek-a-vue

materials and tools

Shoe box or any cardboard box of approximately the same dimensions, light cardboard, colored construction paper, glue, colors for decorating.

procedure

1. Using paper and light cardboard, cut out trees, flowers, houses, animals, people, or whatever is needed for parts of the picture that is to be developed within the box. Color them and glue them in place in an upright position within the box. Place them so that your picture has depth. Keep the scene within the back three-quarters of the box. The sides and back end of the box should be painted or finished to add depth and size to the picture (Fig. 1).
2. In the lid cut two or three openings that will reflect the outside light upon the important features of your scene. Place the lid upon the box (Fig. 2).
3. In the front of the box cut a round peephole about the size of a half dollar (Fig. 2). To use, close one eye and hold the peephole to the other eye. Be sure to have good overhead light.

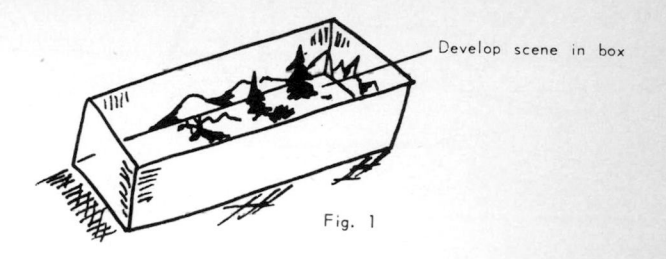

Develop scene in box

Fig. 1

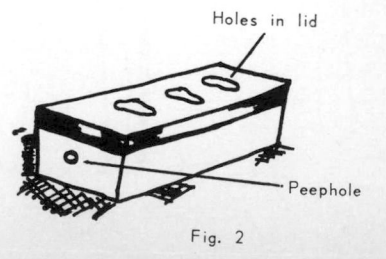

Holes in lid

Peephole

Fig. 2

see seeds grow

materials and tools

Two pieces of glass the same size, approximately 4 by 6 in., piece of paper toweling, two elastic bands, clothes hanger wire or other pliable wire, tin-foil pie plate, canary seeds, pliers.

procedure

1. Cut paper towel the size of the glass and place on top of one of the pieces of glass. Sprinkle seeds on towel and place the second piece of glass on top. Hold together firmly with elastic bands stretched across either end (Fig. 1).
2. Bend wire into a shape that will hold the glass upright. Be sure the glass is somewhat larger than the holder so that it will rest against the wire and not slip off at any point (Fig. 2).
3. Place glass in holder and set it in the pie plate half filled with water. The water will seep up through the paper and provide the moisture to make the seeds sprout above the glass. Canary seeds grow very quickly. Be sure to keep water in the pan at all times so the seeds remain moist.

average time required

30 minutes

203

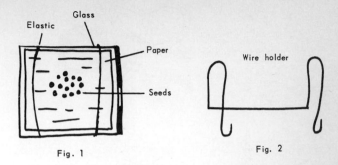

Fig. 1

Fig. 2

Fig. 3

simple string chain

materials and tools

Heavy twine.

procedure

1. Take a 3-ft. piece of twine and tie it to a doorknob or the corner of a chair (Fig. 1).
2. Make a slipknot just below where the twine is tied (Figs. 2 and 3).
3. To make the chain put the first and second fingers of your left hand through the loop of the slipknot (Fig. 4). Grasp the string at point B with the two fingers and pull it through loop A. The right hand holds to the end of the string and allows a few inches of the cord to go through loop A. After the new loop is formed through loop A, hold the right hand steady and continue pulling new formed loop with the left hand. (Do not allow more string to enter loop.) This tightens the original loop A and forms a slipknot around the bottom of the new loop.
4. You now have another loop, so continue reaching through, looping, and pulling it into a knot until you have a chain.
5. To finish the chain so that it will not unravel, pull the main string through the last loop and draw the string tight. This will form a knot (Fig. 4).

15 minutes for a 36-in. chain

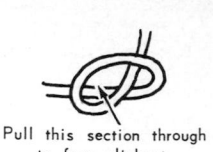

Fig. 1

Pull this section through
to form slipknot

Fig. 2

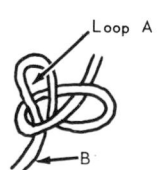

Loop A

B

Fig. 3

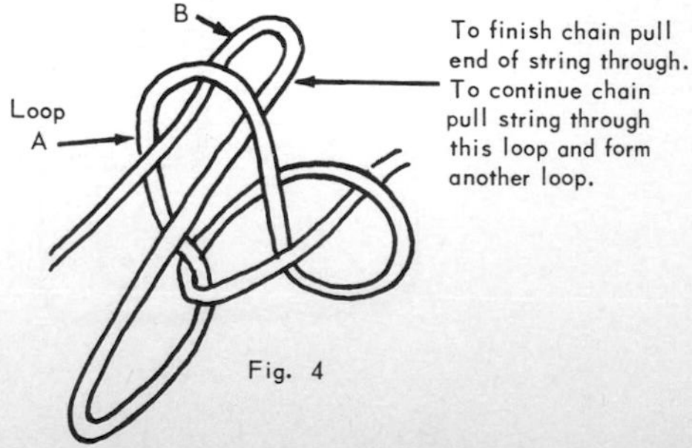

B

Loop
A

To finish chain pull
end of string through.
To continue chain
pull string through
this loop and form
another loop.

Fig. 4

soap carving

materials and tools

Bar of soft-textured soap, sharp knife, toothpick.

procedure

1. Draw the desired pattern on a piece of paper. Trace the pattern on both sides of the soap, making sure they match.
2. Deepen the pattern lines with a toothpick or sharp instrument.
3. Follow pattern and cut out design. First, cut off the extra parts of soap and corners (Fig. 1). Next, use very small strokes and cut out little pieces until you have the desired shape. Hollow out sections around the arms and between the legs. Make the delicate features last (Fig. 2).
4. Dip your fingers in water and rub the soap lightly to smooth it.

average time required

60 minutes

Cut off corners along dotted lines

Fig. 1

Fig. 2

spool dolls

materials and tools

Spool, cloth scraps, sponge or foam plastic, felt scraps, thread, needle, yarn, decorating materials.

procedure

1. Use the sponge or plastic foam to make a ball large enough for the head and place it on top of the spool (Fig. 1).
2. Place a square of cloth large enough to cover the entire doll over the head. Tie a piece of yarn around the bottom of the head and at the waist (Fig. 2).
3. Cut hands and arms from the felt material and sew them in place (Figs. 2 and 3).
4. Add features, clothing, yarn hair, then decorate as desired (Fig. 4).

average time required

40 minutes

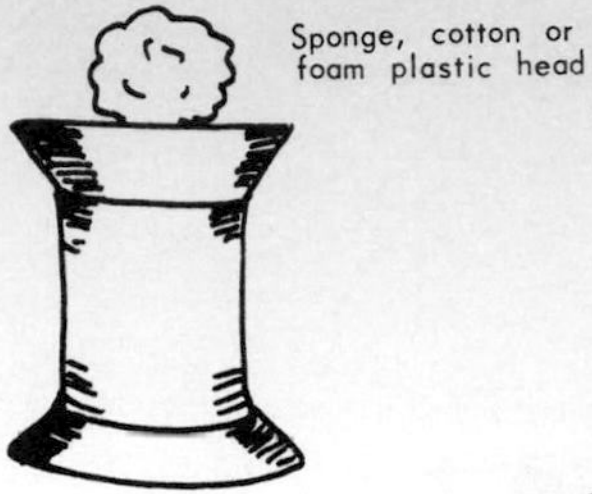

Sponge, cotton or foam plastic head

Fig. 1

Fig. 2

Fig. 3

Yarn

Fig. 4

tie rack

materials and tools

One piece of wood about 8 in. long, ½ to ¾ in. thick, and 6 in. wide, five 2-in. nails, sandpaper, screw hook.

procedure

1. Sand the block of wood with the grain, until smooth.
2. Drive three nails about ½ in. deep into the face of the block and at about a 45° angle. Space as in Fig. 1.
3. Drive a nail into each side of the block at approximately the same angle as in procedure 2. Space the nails as in Fig. 1.
4. Screw the ring into the top of the tie rack (Fig. 2).
5. Paint or stain the block of wood. Allow the paint to dry before using.

average time required

40 minutes plus the time required to decorate and dry.

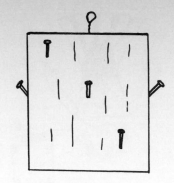

Fig. 1

Side view

Fig. 2

twisted-crepe-paper vase

materials and tools

Crepe paper, glue, small glass jar or plastic liquid detergent bottle with its neck trimmed off, scissors.

procedure

1. Cut the crepe paper into strips 1½ in. wide (Fig. 1).
2. Fasten one end of the crepe-paper strip to a chair, or have someone hold it. Twist the strip into a cord about ¼ in. in diameter. An easy way to twist the crepe paper is to fasten the free end of the paper to a hand drill or open end of an egg beater, then turn the drill or beater.
3. Place glue on the bottom of the jar and glue the crepe paper by laying it in a flat circle (Fig. 2).
4. After covering the bottom of the bottle with crepe paper, continue up the sides until you reach the top of the jar. When you reach the end of one crepe-paper strip, taper the end of the strip with scissors and glue it to the next section (Figs. 3 and 4).

average time required

60 minutes

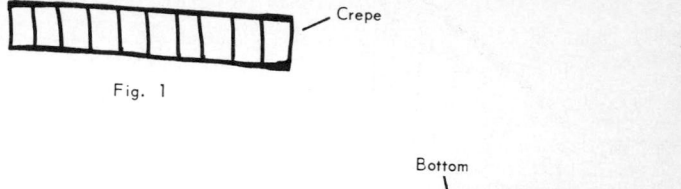

Cut off 1 1/2" strips

Crepe

Fig. 1

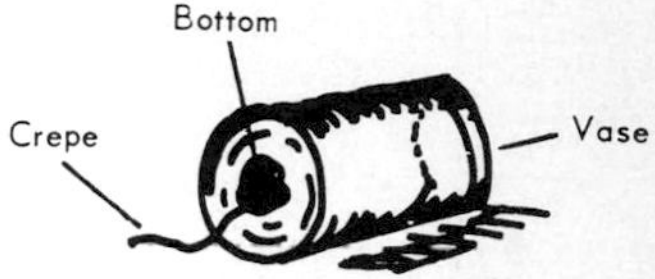

Bottom

Crepe

Vase

Fig. 2

Fig. 3

Fig. 4

208

wriggly dragon

materials and tools

Five blocks of plastic foam varying in size up to 2½ in. square, needle, cord, shingle nails, cardboard, two small colored buttons, straight pins, sandpaper, cutting blade, crayons or colors.

procedure

1. Cut the blocks into the body sections. Sand and smooth the sections.
2. Cut five pieces of jagged or saw-edged cardboard to fit the top edge of each body piece. Make a slit in the top edge of each body piece and slip the jagged edges into place.
3. Run a cord thread through the sections, sewing them together.
4. On the head section fasten the two button eyes with straight pins. Place two nails into the top of the head to resemble antennae. For legs, push nails into the sides of each body section. Using crayons or dry felt ink markers, decorate and color the dragon (Fig. 1).

40 minutes or longer, depending upon the amount of decorating and coloring.

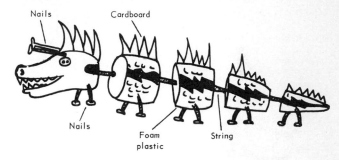

Fig. 1

part six   sixth-grade ages

sixth-grade ages

Box-of-many-faces **213**

Christmas Candles **215**

Crepe-paper Lei **216**

Elusive Elastic Trick **217**

Foam Pins and Ornaments **219**

Folded Newspaper Hat **220**

Folded Tissue Carnation **222**

Identification Tag **223**

Lively Mouse **224**

Marble Bag or Girl's Purse **226**

Marble Game **229**

Miniature Bowling Blocks **231**

Miniature Shuffle-board **232**

Mystery Wheel **234**

Paper Tree **236**

Perpetual Motion Sunray Motor **237**

Plaster of Paris Splash **239**

Reading Stand **241**

Rickrack Earrings **242**

Schoolbook Strap **243**

Spool Tractor **244**

Tippy **245**

Walnut-shell Picture **246**

Wire Necklace or Belt **247**

Yarn Ball, Method One **249**

Yarn Ball, Method Two **250**

box-of-many-faces

materials and tools

Cardboard cleanser or salt container, a soda pop can, white paper, paints or felt dry ink marker, ruler, cutting blade.

procedure

1. Cut the cardboard container down to the same length as the soda pop can, which is usually 5 in. tall (Fig. 1). Leave the bottom in the cardboard can. If the pop can doesn't fit firmly in the cleanser can, glue a few strips of paper around the pop can until the proper fit is obtained.
2. Cut a piece of clean white paper into a section 9 by 5 in. This sheet should just fit around the outside of the cleanser can. Lay this paper on the table and draw three face-shaped ovals as shown in Fig. 2. Be sure the three ovals are identical in their dimensions and positions on the paper. The ovals should be made about 4½ in. high and 2 in. wide at the widest point.
3. With lightly drawn lines, divide the strip of paper horizontally into four sections, each section being 1¼ in. (Fig. 2).
4. In the top sections draw the forehead, hair, and a hat, if desired. In section two draw the eyebrows, eyes, and ears.

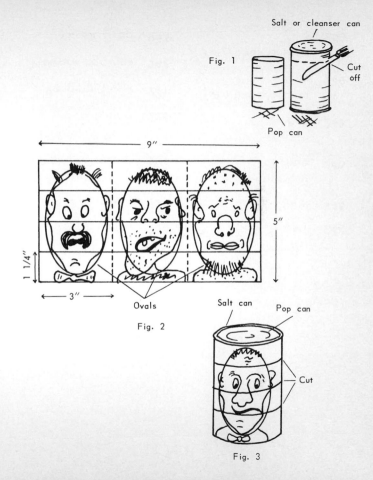

Salt or cleanser can

Fig. 1

Cut off

Pop can

Ovals

Fig. 2

Salt can

Pop can

Cut

Fig. 3

213

In the third section draw the nose and mouth, and in the bottom section the chin, shoulders, and tie. The nose can be placed in the third section if you prefer. Vary the features as much as possible, but be sure to keep them in their restricted areas. Color the faces as desired.

5. Glue the strip of paper with the faces around the cleanser can.
6. Place the soda pop can inside the cleanser can and, using a sharp blade, cut along each of the three lightly drawn lines, separating the cleanser can into four equal parts (Fig. 3).
7. Twist the bands forward or backward and you will develop many different faces.

average time required

90 minutes, depending upon the time spent developing the faces.

christmas candles

materials and tools

Old candles, milk carton, pencil, stove or hot plate.

procedure

1. Melt down the old candles by placing them in the top of a double boiler or in a small pan placed in a larger pan containing water.
2. When the candles are melted, remove the wicks and save them for future use.
3. Cut a milk carton down to the height you desire for your candle (Fig. 1).
4. Fill the carton with melted wax.
5. Tie a wick around the center of a pencil and place the pencil across the top of the carton in such a way that the wick hangs down into the center of the wax (Fig. 2).
6. When the wax has cooled and hardened, tear away the milk carton.
7. Multi-colored candles can be made by dribbling different colored waxes on top of each other over the candle. To color the wax, add crayons to the melting wax.

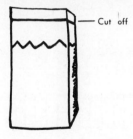

Fig. 1

Fig. 2

crepe-paper lei

materials and tools

Crepe paper, thread, needle, pinking shears if available.

procedure

1. Mark the roll of crepe paper into sections 1½ in. wide and cut off the sections with pinking shears (Fig. 1).
2. Thread the needle with a double thread 4 ft. long and tie a large knot in the end.
3. Sew down the center of a strip of crepe paper using a ¼-in. running stitch (Fig. 2). As you sew, gather the crepe paper against the knot.
4. After you have sewn several strips of crepe paper in this manner, hold firmly to the end of the thread and crepe with your left hand and with your right twist the paper clockwise until it forms a smooth roll. As the roll forms, move your left hand up the roll, keeping close to the twisting area (Fig. 3).
5. Complete enough strips to make the desired length, then tie both ends of the thread to form the circle (Fig. 4).
6. If you wish a multi-colored lei, use several colors of crepe paper, or sew two different colors of crepe back to back with the running stitch to form a two-toned lei.

average time required

30 to 60 minutes, depending upon the length of the lei. A short wrist lei will require about 30 minutes. Caution children about the use of the needle when using a long thread. Teach them to keep the needle close to their work and to set the needle down after several running stitches to pull the thread through with their fingers.

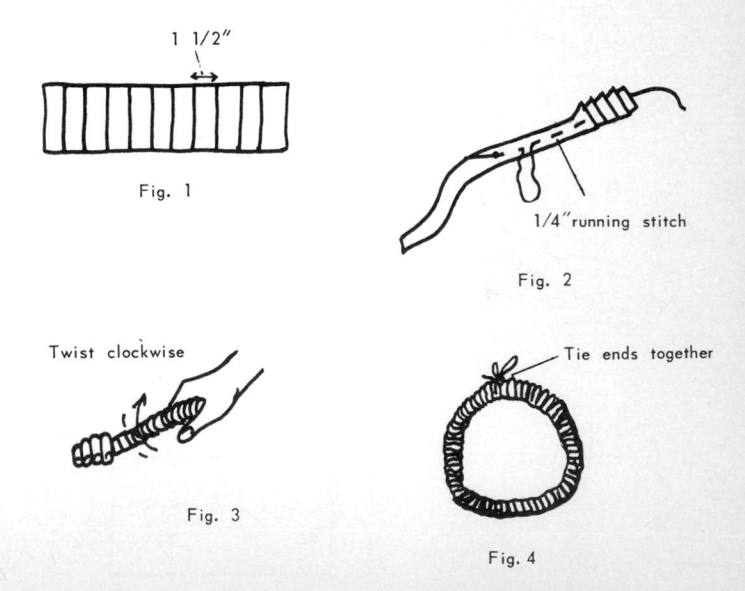

1 1/2"

Fig. 1

1/4" running stitch

Fig. 2

Twist clockwise

Fig. 3

Tie ends together

Fig. 4

elusive elastic trick

materials and tools

A piece of wood 1½ by 1½ by 3 in., a short piece of wood about 1 in. square, and a piece of wood ⁵⁄₁₆ in. in diameter and 4 in. long, pocket knife, wood drill ⁵⁄₁₆ in., glue, elastic band.

procedure

1. Drill a ⁵⁄₁₆ in. hole lengthwise through the center of the 3-in. long piece of wood (Fig. 1).
2. Cut a ¾-in. length from the round piece of wood, making sure that it will fit the hole you have made in the other wood. Place a piece of elastic in the hole so that it can be seen from both inside the hole and the outside end, then glue in the ¾-in. plug to hold the elastic.
3. From the small square piece of wood whittle a snapper head as in Fig. 2. Make it cone-shaped with smooth, rounding edges so it will slip easily through your fingers when squeezed. Drill a hole in the wide end of the snapper head and fit a piece of the round wood into it, leaving 2 in. protruding. Cut a notch about ⅛ in. from the end of the protruding wood (Fig. 2).
4. The trick is to deceive the observers into thinking you can, and have, snagged the elastic inside the hole on the notched

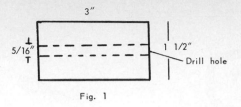

Fig. 1

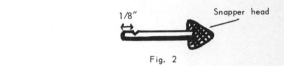

Fig. 2

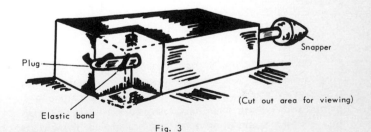

Fig. 3

217

end of the snapper. When they try, if they do not know the trick, they find it impossible.

Solution: Hold the tapered end of the snapper between the thumb and the first finger and place the notched end into the hole with the elastic (Fig. 3). Twist it around and pull up on it to give the impression you are trying to catch the elastic on the hook. When the onlookers are sufficiently impressed with the difficulty of the operation, decide that you have caught the elastic and start to pull the snapper out of the hole. After you have pulled it out about 1 in., squeeze the snapper head so that it snaps back into the hole. To the observers it looks as if the elastic has caught and pulled the snapper back into the hole.

average time required

90 minutes

foam pins and ornaments

materials and tools

A small block of foam plastic, small safety pin, knife, sandpaper, adhesive tape, needles, thread, thumbtacks, decorative materials (buttons, beads, yarn, fur, felt).

procedure

1. From the foam block cut out a section ½ in. thick, 1¼ in. wide and 1½ in. long (Fig. 1).
2. With the knife, round off the edges and shape the foam as desired. Use sandpaper to smooth and finish the block (Fig. 2).
3. Develop the face and features, using buttons or thumbtacks for the eyes, beads for a mouth, felt for ears, and yarn or fur for hair (Fig. 3). You can design any shaped ornament you wish, such as stars, diamonds, or flowers.
4. On the back of the pin sew or tape in place a small safety pin (Fig. 4). If you wish a chain ornament instead of a pin, insert a screw eye in the top of the foam art.

average time required

40 minutes

219

Fig. 1

Fig. 2

Fig. 3

Fig. 4

folded newspaper hat

materials and tools

A sheet of wrapping paper or newspaper, crayons or felt dry ink markers.

procedure

1. Cut the paper to be 30 by 24 in. This will make a size 7 to 7¼ hat. Change the proportions of your paper sheet to make a smaller or larger hat.
2. Place the sheet of paper flat on a table and fold A to B as in Fig. 1.
3. Fold the corners C and D to the middle point of paper, forming a pyramid as in Figs. 2 and 3.
4. Separate the top and bottom flaps and fold the top flap E upward twice. First, fold it in half on the dotted line, then fold it so the first fold is even with the bottom edge formed by the C and D sections. This places the double-folded E flap over the bottom edge of the C and D sections (Fig. 3).
5. Fold the pyramid formed by the C and D sections forward and down and tuck the point of the pyramid under the E flap (Figs. 3 and 4).
6. Turn the hat over and fold sections G and H inward as in Figs. 5 and 6.

7. Fold flap F in half along the dotted line, then fold it again and tuck the upper half of it over flap E (Figs. 6 and 7).
8. If you want a hat that is more rounded, fold corners J and K down to the bottom rim flap and tuck the points securely underneath (Figs. 7 and 8).
9. Color or decorate the hat with crayons or felt dry ink markers.

average time required

20 minutes

folded tissue carnation

materials and tools

One facial tissue (regular size), bobby pin, piece of green crepe paper 4 by ½ in.

procedure

1. Fold the tissue in half, then fold again to form a small square. Cut along both folded edges (Fig. 1.) If a fringed carnation is desired, fringe two opposite sides of the square (Fig. 2).
2. Fold the tissue like an accordion, making the folds about ½ in. apart (Fig. 3). Be sure the fringes are at the ends.
3. Press the folded tissue together and place a bobby pin around the center (Fig. 4).
4. Spread the tissue out to form a circle, then separate each thin layer to form the petals of the flower (Figs. 5, 6, and 7).
5. Pinch the bobby pin together to form the stem and cover it with green crepe paper. Use glue or Scotch tape to secure the end.

average time required

40 minutes

222

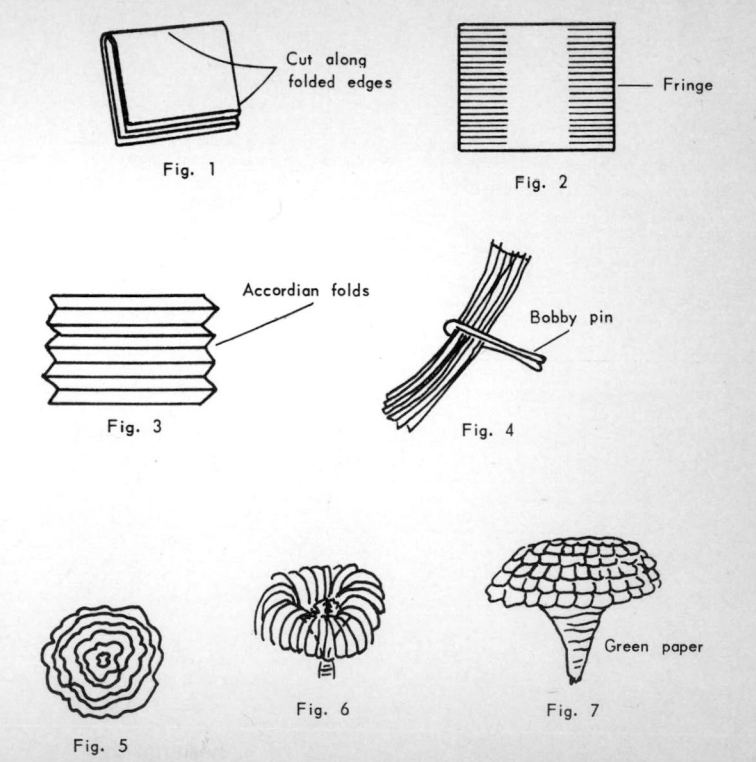

Cut along folded edges

Fig. 1

Fringe

Fig. 2

Accordian folds

Fig. 3

Bobby pin

Fig. 4

Fig. 5

Fig. 6

Green paper

Fig. 7

identification tag

materials and tools

A short branch or piece of pine wood with a 2-in. diameter, shellac or clear varnish, alphabet macaroni, glue, a small chain or cord, fine sandpaper, hand saw or band saw, small drill.

procedure

1. Using the saw, cut off a slice of the limb. Hold the wood at an angle to obtain a more beautiful grain line. Cut the slice about ¼ in. thick (Fig. 1).
2. Sand the faces of the block until they are smooth. Be careful not to break or disturb the bark when you are using a pine bough tag.
3. From the macaroni select the letters of your name and glue them to the face of the block of wood (Fig. 2).
4. After the glue has dried, use a clean cloth to rub in the varnish or shellac. You can use tan or brown wax shoe polish if you wish. This will give your tag a rich color and beautiful polish.
5. Drill a small hole into the tag, place it on a cord or chain, and wear it around your neck or wrist (Fig. 2).

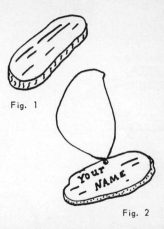

Fig. 1

Fig. 2

223

lively mouse

materials and tools

One half of a walnut shell, black yarn, glue, felt, small piece of round wood, elastic band, black thread, black ink, metal nut or washer, hand drill.

procedure

1. Cut out a small rod of wood similar to a spool. Cut the spool small so that it will fit easily inside the walnut shell (Fig. 1).
2. Cut two equally spaced notches adjacent to each other at each end of the spool and run an elastic band lengthwise around the spool (Fig. 2).
3. Drill two small holes on each side of the walnut shell close to the edge, and one hole in the top of the shell (Fig. 3).
4. Wrap thread around the spool and over the elastic band at least fifteen times (Fig. 2).
5. Cut the ends of the elastic band and, placing the spool inside of the shell, push the ends of the elastic band through the drilled holes and tie on the outside of the shell (Figs. 1 and 3).
6. Run the thread through the hole in the top of the shell (Fig. 3).
7. Cut two little ears from felt or other heavy material and glue to the shell as in Fig. 3.

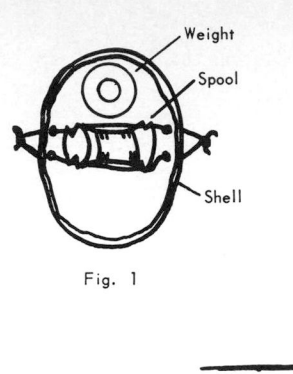

Fig. 1

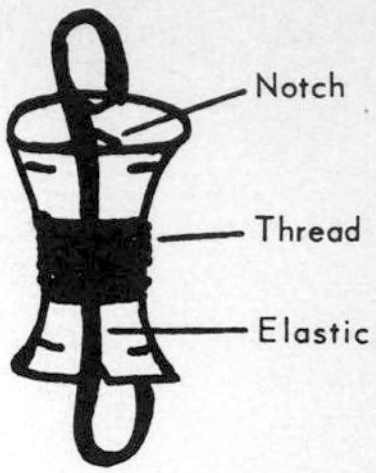

Fig. 2

Fig. 3

Fig. 4

8. Glue black thread on the nose for whiskers and a piece of black yarn on the back for a tail. Mark the other features with black ink (Fig. 3).

9. To operate, place the mouse on the floor and pull up and down on the thread. Do not worry if this action lifts the mouse off the floor. When the hand is lowered, the thread re-winds on the spool and the mouse runs forward. The upward pull should unwind the thread and wind the elastic band. If the mouse is too light to accomplish this, glue a metal nut or washer on the inside of the shell as in Fig. 1.

10. For variation, a turtle may be made instead of a mouse, as in Fig. 4. Make the turtle's head and feet from paper.

average time required

120 minutes

marble bag or girl's purse

materials and tools

A piece of medium-heavy cardboard 5 by 6 in., strong string or cord, yarn or colored cord, scissors, bobby pin or weaving needle.

procedure

1. Measure and mark the cardboard loom as shown in Figs. 1 and 2.
2. At the top and bottom cut a slit ⅛ in. deep at each marked interval (Fig. 2).
3. To make the loom, start the string at point A and bring it down the face of the cardboard to position *a*. Run the string through slit *a* and bring it up the back of the board to position A and tie it securely at this point (Fig. 2).
4. Bring the cord through A and across the front of the board and back through slit B. Take it down the back of the board to *b*. Run the cord through slit *b* and bring it up the front of the board to B. Run the cord through slit B and across the back of the board to slit C. Bring the string through slit C to the front of the board. Continue this process until you reach point *t* at the bottom of the loom (Fig. 2). At this point loop the cord around the ⅛-in. bottom tab of cardboard and tie it securely on itself. Leave a few inches of loom

Fig. 1

string hanging to tie onto the weaving yarn (Figs. 2 and 3). If you have threaded your loom correctly, you will have nineteen strings on the front and twenty on the back.

5. Tie the weaving yarn to the piece of string at *t* and, using an over and under weaving method, weave across the board from right to left. Upon reaching the left side of the loom, continue around the left edge of the loom and weave across the back. Be sure that you continue the over and under method at all times, making sure that you go over or under as needed when you turn the yarn from one side of the board to the other. As you weave, keep pushing the finished part tightly to the bottom of the loom, keeping it tight and even all the way to the top.

6. To finish, tie the yarn securely to one of the loom cords at the top of the loom. To make the draw cords, weave a ribbon, heavy cord, or several strands of yarn through the loom cords about ½ in. from the top of the purse and tie the ends together (Fig. 4).

7. To remove the purse, slip the strings from around the top tabs and, holding the cardboard with your left hand and the purse with your right, slide the purse from the cardboard.

average time required

90 minutes, depending upon the design. You can use differently colored yarns while weaving or sew in a design after

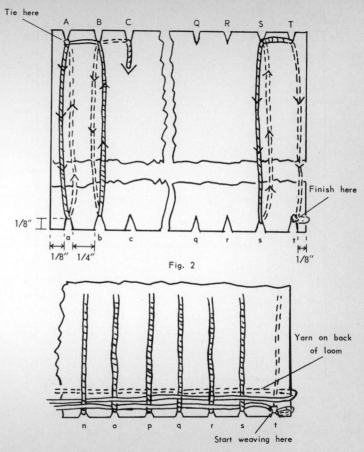

Fig. 2

Fig. 3

227

the bag is finished. It is a good idea to weave in two draw cords, bringing one from each side of the bag.

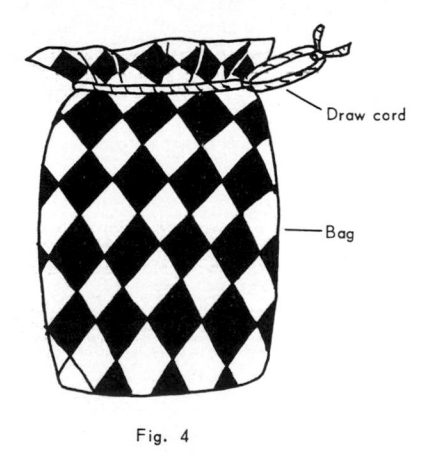

Draw cord

Bag

Fig. 4

marble game

materials and tools

A piece of ½-in. plywood, small finishing nails, marbles, saw, pine wood, hammer.

procedure

1. Saw a piece of plywood 10 by 12 in. (Fig. 1).
2. Saw two strips of pine wood 13 in. long, 1¼ in. wide, and ¼ in. thick. These are for the sides of the board. Also cut a glance board if desired (Fig. 3).
3. Saw two strips of pine wood 10 in. long, 1¼ in. wide, and ¼ in. thick for the ends.
4. Glue and nail these four pieces of wood onto the base piece so they are flush with the bottom of the base and stick up above it ¾ in. (It is better to have these sides and shooting slots made of pine as the edges can be sanded, better to prevent slivers) (Fig. 3).
5. Cut a piece of pine wood 1 in. wide, ¼ in. thick, and 4 in. long and nail and glue it in the lower right-hand corner ¾ in. from the right side board. This is called the shooting slot for the marbles (Fig. 3).
6. Draw the diagram shown in Fig. 4 on the base board. Hammer the nails in place until they stick up about one half inch. The nails are spaced about ⅜ in. apart. The spaces

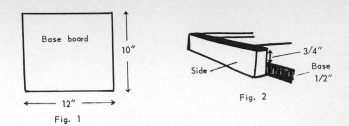

Fig. 1

Fig. 2

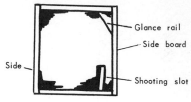

Fig. 3

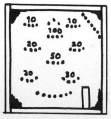

Fig. 4

must be narrow enough to prevent the marbles from slipping through. Mark the scores on the base board with ink or pencil. For a glance board at the right top of the game, you can use a small piece of pine board as mentioned in procedure 2 or hammer in several small nails as shown in Fig. 4.

7. To make the marbles roll to the bottom of the board, place the top of the board on a magazine or thin book, or glue a piece of wood to the bottom of the top edge about 1 in. wide, 1 in. thick, and 8 in. long.

8. *Rules of the game:* Each person shoots all six of his marbles for his inning. A full game is ten innings. Place the marbles in the shooting slot with your index finger behind the first one and flip it out toward the top of the board. The object is to get the marbles to settle in a cup instead of rolling to the bottom of the board where no score is given. After a player has shot his six marbles and totaled his points for that inning, it is the next player's turn. As many players as desired can play, each playing one inning at a time. The winner is the one with the most points at the end of the ten innings.

average time required

180 minutes

miniature bowling blocks

materials and tools

A stick of pine wood 1 in. square, paint, ink or crayon, sandpaper, saw.

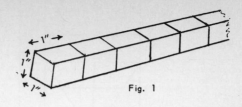

Fig. 1

procedure

1. Cut ten cubes from the stick of pine wood, each 1 by 1 by 1 in. (Fig. 1).
2. Sand the blocks until they are smooth.
3. Paint, or draw with ink, a bowling pin on one side of each block (Fig. 2).
4. To play, place all ten of the blocks in your hands and shake, then throw or roll them at one time upon the table. The blocks which come up with the bowling pin on the top are considered still standing. If all ten pins are down, it is scored as a strike. The blocks with the pins showing on top are thrown again as in regular bowling, two throws for one complete turn. The scoring is the same as in regular bowling with strikes, spares, and so on.

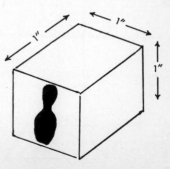

Fig. 2

average time required

30 minutes

miniature shuffleboard

materials and tools

A board 7 to 8 in. wide, ½ in. thick, and 40 in. long (heavy cardboard may be used instead of a board), six black and six red checkers, india ink or enamel paint.

procedure

1. Sand the board until smooth.
2. Draw the pattern on the board (Fig. 1).
3. Follow the rules for shuffleboard.
   a. To advance the checkers flip them with your finger.
   b. A player can flip the disk as strongly or as lightly as he likes, but if it doesn't pass the dead line or if it passes the minus-10-point area, the disk must be taken off the board. The disk must be played from the serving area.
   c. The game may be played as singles or doubles. If you play singles, clear the board and return the checkers to the players after each set. Do not turn the board or change ends. In the doubles game place partners at opposite ends of the board.
   d. All disks are placed at one end, with the two players having their own colored disks. They take turns until the twelve disks have been played.

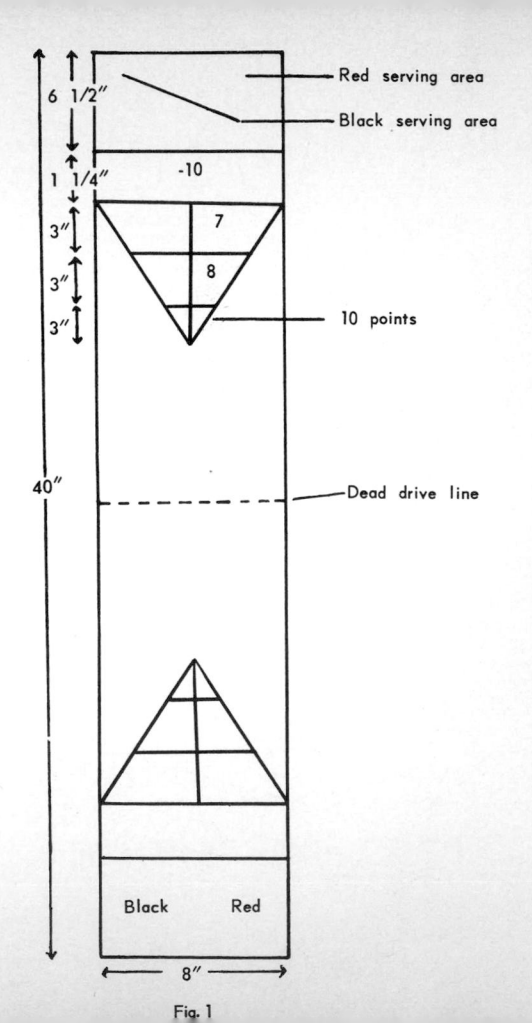

Fig. 1

e. When all the disks have been played, the points are added and the partners at the other end of the board have their turns. Points are given only at the end of the inning, when all of the disks have been played, and are awarded according to their positions at the end of this time. It is permissible to hit the disks during the inning and move them.

f. If a disk comes to rest on a line, the player is awarded the higher of the two possible points. If the disk is touching a line of the 10-points-off area at the end of the inning, ten points are taken from the player's score.

g. The game ends when a predetermined score or number of innings is reached. A game usually consists of 51 points.

average time required

40 minutes

mystery wheel

materials and tools

Two 6-in. foil or paper plates; four pegs 3 in. long made from soft, lightweight wood; two elastic bands; a lead weight or metal nut; two matches or toothpicks; crayons or felt dry ink markers.

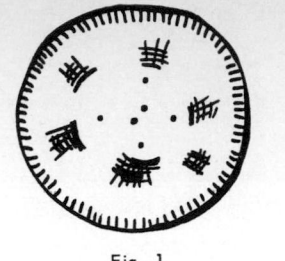

Fig. 1

Fig. 2

Pegs

Thumbtacks

procedure

1. With the crayons or ink markers decorate the plates as desired.
2. On the inside of each plate mark off four equally spaced points 2 in. from the center of the plate as in Fig. 1.
3. With the pencil marks as guides, use thumbtacks and fasten the sticks in place as in Figs. 2 and 3.
4. Make two holes about ½ in. apart in the center of each plate. Push an elastic band through each hole in one of the plates and place a match between the ends of the elastic band on the bottom side of the plate to prevent them from slipping back through the plate (Fig. 4). Take the elastic bands across the inside of the wheel and push the end of each one through the corresponding holes in the other plate and fasten the ends with a match on the bottom of the plate as before.

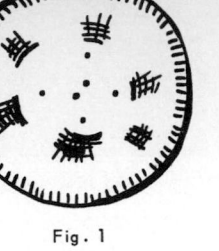

Pegs
Elastic
Match
Weight
Thumbtacks

Fig. 3

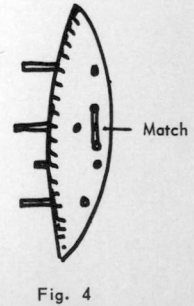

Match

Fig. 4

5. Fasten the weight at the center of one of the elastic bands (Fig. 3).
6. To operate the mystery wheel roll it across the floor. This forward action winds the elastic bands. When the wheel stops going forward, the elastic bands will start to unwind and this will reverse the wheel so it will return to its original position.

average time required

60 minutes

paper tree

materials and tools

Newspaper, string, glue or paste, razor blade or scissors, pencil or rod.

procedure

1. Using a pencil or rod as a core, roll several single sheets of newspaper (15 by 23 in.) one after another until the roll becomes approximately 1 in. in diameter (Fig. 1). Roll the first sheet to within 4 in. of the end of the paper, then place the second sheet over the unrolled part of the first sheet and paste them together.
2. Paste down the edge of the last sheet, or tie it with string or an elastic band (Fig. 1).
3. Remove the pencil and cut three evenly spaced slits around the tube. Cut down about two-thirds of the length of the tube (Fig. 1).
4. Bend down each section (Fig. 2).
5. Place your forefinger into the top of the tube and, twisting clockwise, slowly pull up on the paper tube and each layer of paper will slide up and form the tree (Fig. 3).

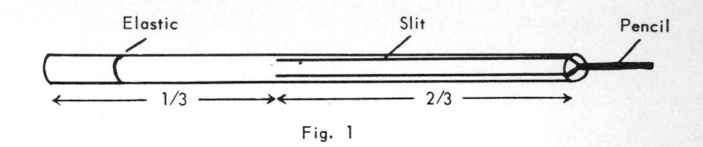

Fig. 1

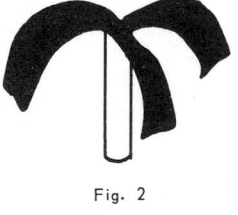

Fig. 2

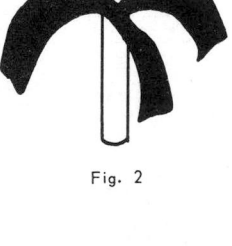

Fig. 3

perpetual motion sunray motor

materials and tools

One ring of an embroidery hoop or any solid, lightweight cardboard ring with a diameter of 7 to 8 in., a sewing needle approximately 2 in. long, three elastic bands ⅛ in. wide and 6 to 7 in. in circumference, two glass tumblers the same size, a sheet of white cardboard about 10 by 10 in. covered with a sheet of tinfoil and adhesive or Scotch tape.

procedure

1. Stretch three elastic bands across the diameter of the hoop like spokes, making sure they all cross at the center. Place the needle through the center as an axle.
2. On a flat surface near a sunlighted window set the two tumblers about ¾ in. apart and even with each other.
3. Place two pieces of tape ⅛ in. apart over the rim edge of each glass. This tape forms a groove for the needle axle. The grooves should be placed opposite one another. Set the sunray wheel in place with the axle extending from glass to glass and resting in the grooves formed by the tape.
4. Balance the wheel. Give it a gentle push. If the wheel oscillates back and forth with the heavier portion of the

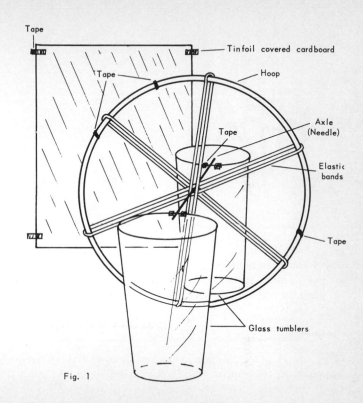

Tape

Tinfoil covered cardboard

Tape

Hoop

Tape

Axle (Needle)

Elastic bands

Tape

Glass tumblers

Fig. 1

wheel resting at the bottom, wrap a narrow band of tape around the rim at the top of the wheel until it balances. It is important that this be done carefully so that the wheel will turn smoothly.

5. Slowly turn the wheel while standing in front of it and watch for uneven sideward alignment. If it is out of alignment and wobbles as it turns, the axle is not perpendicular to the rim. Readjustment of the tension in one side of one or more of the elastic bands should quickly straighten the axle.

6. Test the motor by placing an illuminated 100-watt bulb as close as possible to one side of the wheel and between the axle and the rim. The heat from the globe should turn the wheel at the rate of about three to five revolutions per minute. If it works smoothly, it is now ready to be run by the rays from the sun.

7. Turn the wheel sideways to the window. Sunlight must shine only on one half of the wheel. With tape fasten the piece of foil-covered cardboard in the window to shade half the motor. The tinfoil will reflect the sun's heat away from one half of the motor and also shade it. In full or bright sunlight the motor should turn at about the same speed as when run by the light globe. The wheel should operate as long as the sun shines on it. The motor operates because the heat shortens the elastic bands on one side of the motor while the other side, which is in shadow, is cooler and, therefore, lengthens the bands. The stretching and tightening of the bands change the weight of the sides of the wheel and, therefore, cause it to turn slowly as the heavy side rotates to the bottom. By the time the heated spokes move to the shadowed side, they lengthen again, while the other spokes coming into position in the sunlight's heat shorten to keep the wheel turning.

average time required

30 to 60 minutes, depending upon the amount of time required to balance and align the motor. It requires only a few minutes to assemble and put in operation once it has been balanced.

plaster of paris splash

materials and tools

A piece of black, white, or pink net, 9 by 12 in. (you can use an old curtain), a piece of colored construction paper 9 by 12 in., a contrasting piece of colored construction paper 9 by 12 in., plaster of paris, water, water colors or paint, glue, spoon or stick (optional), Scotch tape.

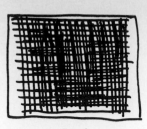

Fig. 1

Fig. 2

procedure

1. Place the net over a piece of the construction paper and secure in place with tape (Fig. 1).
2. Put approximately seven heaping teaspooonfuls of plaster of paris into a small foil dish. Add water, a small amount at a time, mixing until it is thick and creamy.
3. Drop the plaster by spoonfuls so it will splatter on the net. Splashing it on with the fingers will also produce many interesting forms. Be sure the plaster is thin enough so it will splatter when it hits the net and not merely fall in globs. Let the shapes form naturally—do not rub in with the fingers (Fig. 2).
4. Let dry overnight.
5. Turn the picture in all directions until forms or objects can be distinguished. Use your imagination and you will discover many shapes and objects.

Fig. 3

6. Paint the objects, using many bright colors for a pretty effect.
7. Cut a frame from the contrasting construction paper and glue around the edges of the net to complete the picture (Fig. 3).

average time required

40 minutes for the actual working time.

reading stand

materials and tools

A piece of plywood ¼ in. thick, 9 in. wide, and 21 in. long, a piece of soft pine ½ in. thick and 6 by 6 in., small shingle or finishing nails, hammer, sandpaper, ruler.

procedure

1. Cut the plywood into three pieces, 11, 9, and 1 in. in length (Fig. 1).
2. Cut the soft pine in half from corner to corner (Fig. 2).
3. Nail the holder together as in Fig. 3. Sand all of the edges smooth and paint or stain if desired.

average time required

60 minutes

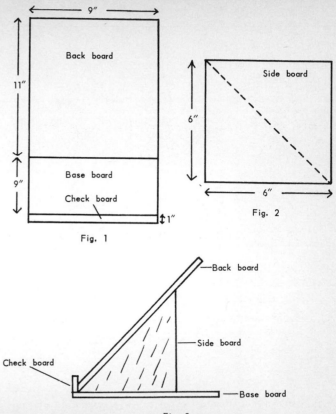

Fig. 1

Fig. 2

Fig. 3

rickrack earrings

materials and tools

Rickrack (the narrow type makes a smaller, prettier earring), cement, needle, thread, scissors, beads, shells or sequins, a pair of earring backs.

procedure

1. Count 25 points on the rickrack and cut off at the next point (Fig. 1).
2. Start sewing by putting the needle through the first point of the rickrack near the edge and back through the second point (Fig. 2). Continue sewing in one point and out the next until you have sewed through all the points.
3. When the sewing is completed, straighten out the rickrack to prevent twisting, then pull it tightly together until it forms a flower. Sew or tie the ends of the thread so they will not pull out (Figs. 3 and 4).
4. Glue a colored bead, shell pearl, or sequin in the center of the flower. Glue the flower to the earring back and let it dry thoroughly before wearing (Fig. 5).

average time required

60 to 80 minutes. The earring backs can be purchased from a variety store.

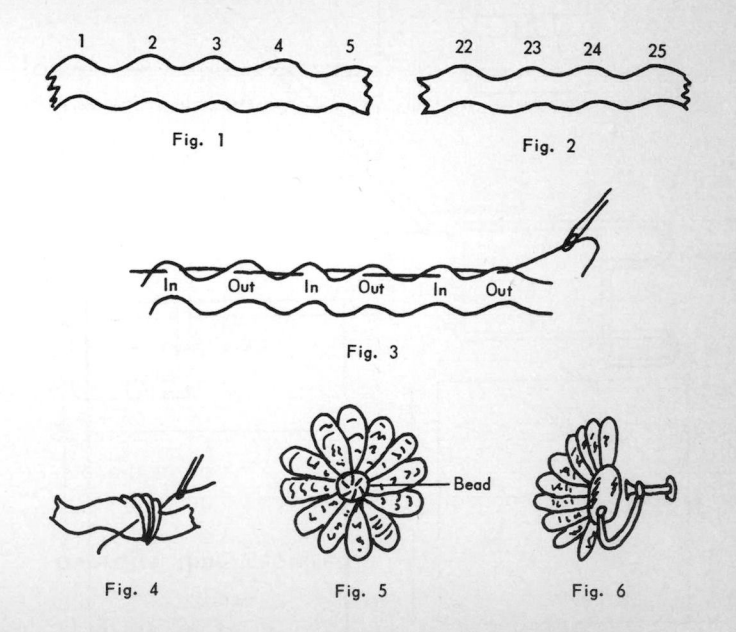

Fig. 1

Fig. 2

Fig. 3

Fig. 4

Fig. 5

Fig. 6

schoolbook strap

materials and tools

Old inner tube, wire clothes hanger, scissors, staples or needle and thread, pliers.

procedure

1. Cut a strip from the inner tube ¾ by 11 in. This length will hold several books.
2. With pliers cut off a 3¼-in. piece of the clothes hanger and bend it into a rectangle measuring ½ in. wide and ¾ in. long. The ends of the wire should overlap about ½ in. (Fig. 1).
3. Cut another piece of clothes hanger 4 in. long and bend it into a rectangle ⅝ in. wide and 2 in. or 2½ in. long. Bend up the end of this rectangle so that it forms a hook which can fasten up through the first wire rectangle you made (Fig. 2).
4. Loop about one inch of the strip of inner tube through each wire rectangle as in Fig. 3. Fasten these ends down by stapling or sewing with needle and thread.
5. To use, wrap the belt around your books and fasten the buckle by hooking the bent end up through the other rectangle (Fig. 4).

6. By using a longer piece of tubing you can make a belt. The belt can be decorated with enamel paints, felt dry ink markers, or designs cut or punched out of the rubber (Fig. 5).

average time required

40 to 60 minutes, depending upon the amount and type of decorations used.

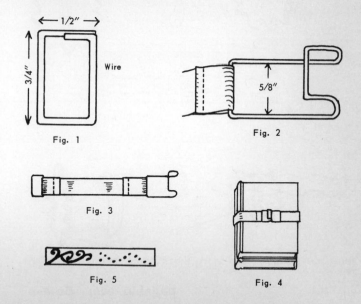

Fig. 1

Fig. 2

Fig. 3

Fig. 5

Fig. 4

spool tractor

materials and tools

One large, empty thread spool, two matchsticks, one elastic band, knife.

procedure

1. With a sharp knife, notch the ends of the spool to resemble tractor wheels (Fig. 1).
2. Cut a groove crossing the hole at one end of the spool and fit a section of one of the matches into it (Figs. 2 and 3).
3. Slide the elastic band through the spool and push the match section through the loop in the end as in Fig. 3.
4. At the other end of the spool push the other whole matchstick through the end of the elastic band as in Fig. 4, making sure that only one end of the match extends beyond the spool edge.
5. Wind the elastic band by twisting the long match in one direction until the elastic band is twisted tightly. Set the spool on a smooth surface and the tractor will move forward.

average time required

30 minutes

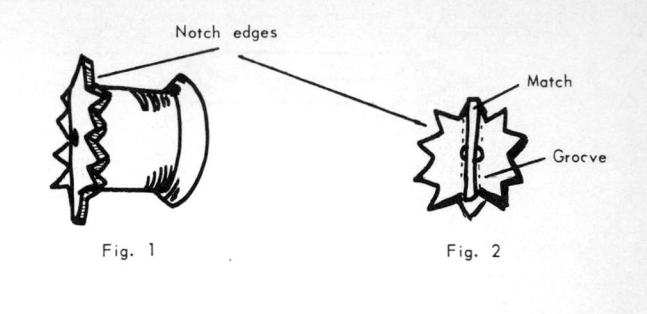

Fig. 1   Fig. 2

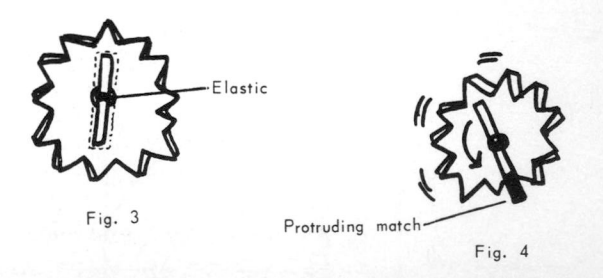

Fig. 3   Fig. 4

tippy

materials and tools

A piece of wood 12 by 6 by 1 in., knife, saw, pencil.

procedure

1. Cut out a paddle as in Fig. 1.
2. From the section of wood saved near the handle of the paddle, cut a piece 1½ in. wide and 5 in. long and taper the ends. This is called the tippy. The tippy also can be made from a round stick, such as a broom handle (Fig. 2).
3. To use, place the tippy on the ground and tap the tapered end with the paddle so it will bounce into the air, then hit it with the paddle. Draw a circle some distance away and see how many hits it takes to get the tippy in the circle. For an exciting racing game, tap the tippy and instead of hitting it while it is in the air, try to catch it on your paddle and run with it. If tippy should fall off the paddle, start over from the beginning.

average time required

60 minutes

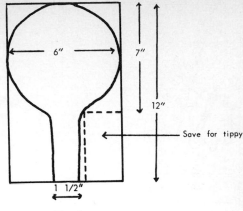

Fig. 1

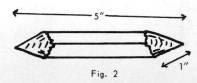

Fig. 2

245

walnut-shell picture

materials and tools

One half of a walnut shell, black yarn, crayons, glue, colored paper.

procedure

1. Glue a sheet of colored paper 4 by 6 in. to the front of a contrasting colored sheet of paper 5 by 7 in., making an even border for a frame.
2. Cut a small feather from a piece of colored paper and glue it to the upper center of the plaque (Fig. 1).
3. Draw an Indian face on the half shell with crayon or ink. Color a band around the head or cut a strip of colored paper and glue it on (Fig. 2).
4. Make hair for the Indian with the black yarn (Fig. 2).
5. Glue the head to the foundation paper so that the feather is above the head as in Fig. 3.

average time required

40 minutes

Fig. 1   Fig. 2

wire necklace or belt

Fig. 1

End

Fig. 2

materials and tools

Fine copper wire, scissors, a short wooden rod, an ornament.

procedure

1. Fashion a rod from a stick or broom handle with a diameter the size you wish to make your chain links (Fig. 1).
2. Cut the wire into strips long enough to encircle the rod twice, with a little left over.
3. Take one piece of wire and bend it into a figure-eight, with the ends in the middle (Fig. 2).
4. Place the wooden rod in one of the loops of wire and, holding the wire between the fingers of the left hand, twist the rod so it will twist the wire. When the wire is twisted three times around itself remove the rod and place it in the other loop. Twist the rod three times in the opposite direction so that you do not unwind the wire. This completes one section of the chain (Fig. 3).
5. To continue the chain, thread a section of wire through the last loop of the preceding link, bend it into a figure-eight, and twist the rod in both loops as before (Fig. 3).
6. Complete the necklace to the length you wish, then form the hook. To make the hook, twist the first loop of a section of wire as before, but do not place the second loop on the

Fig. 3

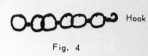

Hook

Fig. 4

Fig. 5

rod. Twist it several times, then bend it together with your fingers and shape it into a hook (Fig. 4).

7. Place the ornament on the chain and fasten it around your neck (Fig. 5). If you desire to make your own ornament, refer to "Foam Pins and Ornaments" or "Identification Tag."

average time required

40 to 60 minutes, depending upon the size of the chain. If you make a chain belt, use heavier wire and pliers for bending and twisting.

yarn ball, method one

materials and tools

A piece of strong cardboard, strong string about 4 in. long, a skein of yarn or several different colors of yarn, pencil, string, compass, scissors.

procedure

1. Draw on the cardboard a circle with a 3½-in. diameter. Cut out the circle. If you desire a bigger or smaller ball, adjust the size of the circle accordingly (Fig. 1).
2. Draw within the center of this circle another circle with the diameter of 1½ in., or larger if you desire a bigger ball. Cut out this circle and you have a doughnut (Fig. 2).
3. Make two of these doughnuts and place them together. Tie the yarn around the doughnut, then begin wrapping. Wrap the yarn around and around the doughnut until the hole in the center is completely filled with yarn. Be sure to use yarn lengths that are easy to handle (Figs. 3 and 4).
4. With scissors or a razor blade cut the yarn between the two doughnuts at their outer edges (Fig. 4). The yarn will fall away from the edge of the doughnut as in Fig. 5.
5. Slightly spread the two cardboard doughnuts and tie a piece of string around the center of the yarn (Fig. 6).

6. Remove the yarn from the doughnut frames.
7. Shape the ball and trim it evenly (Fig. 7).

average time required

40 minutes

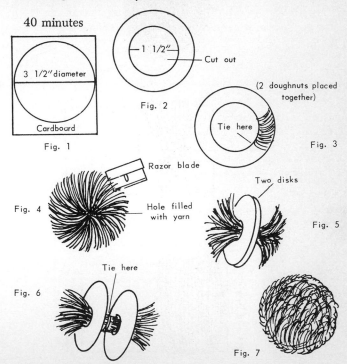

3 1/2" diameter

Cardboard

Fig. 1

1 1/2"

Cut out

Fig. 2

(2 doughnuts placed together)

Tie here

Fig. 3

Razor blade

Fig. 4

Hole filled with yarn

Two disks

Fig. 5

Tie here

Fig. 6

Fig. 7

yarn ball, method two

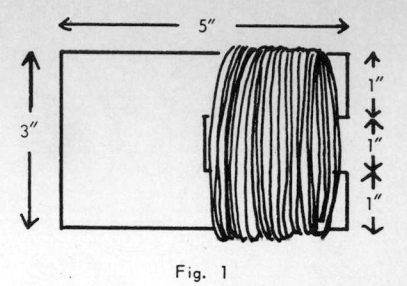

Fig. 1

materials and tools

Same as in "Yarn Ball, Method One."

procedure

1. Make a cardboard frame as shown in Fig. 1.
2. Wind the yarn around the frame about sixty times (Fig. 1). This makes a good-sized ball. If you want a fuller ball, wrap more yarn on the frame. If you want a larger or smaller ball, adjust the size of the frame accordingly.
3. Tie a piece of string around the center of the yarn (Fig. 2).
4. Cut the yarn at the edges as shown in Fig. 2.
5. Remove the yarn from the cardboard. Shape the ball and trim the loose ends (Fig. 3).

average time required

30 minutes

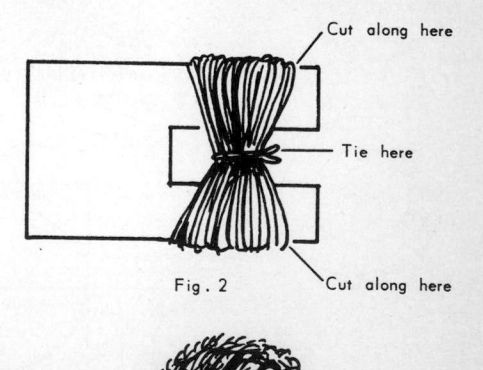

Fig. 2

Fig. 3